Also by Jan Henson Dow

Nonfiction
Writing the Award-Winning Play (with Shannon Michal Dow.)

Poetry
At the Han-ku Pass

Short Plays
Plays that Pop!: One-Act, Ten-Minute, and Monologues

Full-Length Plays
Dark Passages (with Shannon Michal Dow and Robert Schroeder, published by Popular Play Service.)
Dreamers, Shadows, Dreams (with Robert Schroeder, published by Phosphene Publishing Co.)
The Golden Dawn (with Robert Schroeder, published by Phosphene Publishing Co.)
Killing Dante (with Shannon Michal Dow, published by Samuel French, Inc.)
The Magistry (with Robert Schroeder, published by Popular Play Service.)
The Moorlark (with Shannon Michal Dow, published by Phosphene Publishing Co.)
Shaka (with Robert Schroeder, published by Phosphene Publishing Co.)
That Madcap Moon (with Robert Schroeder, published by Phosphene Publishing Co.)

The Moorlark

The Moorlark

A Play by

Jan Henson Dow
&
Shannon Michal Dow

Phosphene Publishing Company
Houston, Texas

The Moorlark
© 2017 by Jan Henson Dow and Shannon Michal Dow
ISBN 10: 0-9851477-8-4
ISBN 13: 978-0-9851477-8-5

This play is a work of fiction. Names, characters, places, and incidents either are products of the author's imagination or are used as fiction.

All rights reserved. No part of this work may be copied or otherwise produced or reproduced in any form—printed, electronic, live performance, videotaping, recording, or otherwise—without express permission of Phosphene Publishing Company, except for brief excerpts used in reviews, articles, and critical works.

Published by
Phosphene Publishing Company
Houston, Texas, USA
phosphenepublishing.com

To Brendan Ward and Ian Ward
and
To the Memory of Scott Dow

Production of The Moorlark

This edition of *The Moorlark* is dedicated to the reading public only. Professionals and amateurs are hereby warned that the play is subject to production fees. All rights, including professional, amateur, motion pictures, recitation, lecturing, public reading, radio broadcasting, television, and the rights of translation into foreign languages, are strictly reserved.

The amateur live stage performance rights to *The Moorlark* are controlled exclusively by Phosphene Publishing Company. There is a fee of $35 to produce this play, and the fee must be paid and rights secured in writing from Phosphene Publishing Company at least two weeks prior to the opening performance of the play. The fee must be paid whether the play is presented for charity or by a non-profit or profit-seeking organization and whether or not admission is charged.

Professional and stock royalty will be quoted on application to Phosphene Publishing Company.

Copying from this book without express permission of the publisher is strictly forbidden by law, and the right of performance is not transferable.

Whenever the play is produced, the following notice must appear on all programs, printing, and advertising for the play: "Produced by special arrangement with Phosphene Publishing Company."

Due authorship credit must be given on all programs, printing, and advertising for the play.

No one shall commit or authorize any act or omission by which the copyright, or the right to copyright, of this play may be impaired.

No one may make any changes to this play in the process of production, or otherwise.

Correspondence and inquiries may be made through the Phosphene Publishing Company website at phosphenepublishing.com.

The Moorlark

Cast of Characters
(In order of appearance)

CHARLOTTE BRONTE has light brown hair, worn in a simple, confined manner. Her appearance is marked by energy and determination. She is 32.

ANNE BRONTE has a sweet, gentle face. She is 26.

THE REV. MR. PATRICK BRONTE is a tall man with an erect carriage and a proud bearing. His face and manner are marked by intelligence and energy. Though he was born in Ireland, there remains only a trace of an Irish accent in his speech.

EMILY BRONTE is slim and has dark hair, worn long and flowing in loose curls, and dark sparkling eyes in a face that mirrors her ever-changing emotions—at one moment gay or willful, at another moment pensive or dreaming. She is an elemental spirit, with a natural magnetism. She is willful and proud, selfish and obstinate, pensive and dreaming by turns, always with an underlying current of conviction and courage. She is a rare and vital human being. She is 29, and her manner of dress is simple and free in contrast to the more conventional costumes of her sisters.

TABBY is the Bronte's housekeeper.

JAMES TAYLOR, a representative from the Bronte sisters' publisher, is tall, handsome, and about 30. He has a confident manner, and his bearing is that of a man who would feel at home in London society.

The REV. MR. ARTHUR NICHOLLS is a kindly, awkward man of indeterminate age. He is Mr. Bronte's steadfast but unimaginative and uninspiring curate. Nicholls' clothing is provincial and quite shabby in appearance. His hair is beginning to grow thin. He wears rimless glasses which tend to slide down his nose, and he does not quite know what to do with his hands, which stick too far out of his sleeves.

BRANWELL BRONTE has dark hair worn long and flashing dark eyes. He has his father's look of intelligence but lacks his father's proud bearing. He conveys the same sense of the elemental natural magnetism as does Emily, but in Branwell, these qualities are counteracted by a self-defeating cynicism that is lacking in Emily. Underlying Branwell's cynical manner is an ever-present suggestion of a suppressed tendency toward violence. He is 30.

LANDLORD of the Black Bull Inn.

NAT is the Landlord's employee at the Black Bull Inn. (Voice only.)

The Moorlark

ACT I: SCENE ONE

(A sitting room in Haworth, the house of the Brontes on the Yorkshire moors. The year is 1848. It is early afternoon of an April day and a fire is burning in the fireplace. CHARLOTTE BRONTE is writing at a desk in a corner.)

ANNE
(Entering.)
Oh, Charlotte—Charlotte! Do you think he will come today? Do you? Do you?

CHARLOTTE
I did mention in my reply that I would be happy to receive him this afternoon.

ANNE
What is Mr. Taylor like? What color are his eyes? What color is his hair? How tall is he? How old?

CHARLOTTE
Heavens, Anne, how can I answer all of those questions? I've never met Mr. Taylor, remember. We have only corresponded a few times. Merely notes of respect from an editor to one of his authors and poets.

ANNE

Do you think Mr. Taylor knows the truth about us?

CHARLOTTE

I have only received two letters from Mr. Taylor. All of the rest were addressed to Ellis Bell, in care of Miss Bronte, and so I gave them, unopened, to Emily. But I think he believes his three authors are all one.

ANNE

Can't you hear the gossip said about us?
        (In a mocking tone.)
"I may be a bit old fashioned, my dear, but *Wuthering Heights* and *Jane Eyre* are a bit too shocking even for the 19th Century!"

CHARLOTTE

Not to mention *Agnes Grey*!
        (Mocking.)
"Can the author possibly be, as is rumored, a woman—the daughter of a country parson? Scandalous!"

ANNE

"Nonsense! Authorship is not the proper sphere for young ladies of gentle upbringing."

CHARLOTTE

"The proper sphere for young ladies, my dear, is Christian charity and good works."

ANNE

Oh, Charlotte, you have done enough charity and good works for two lifetimes. You were so happy in Brussels.

CHARLOTTE

Was I happy? I don't remember.

ANNE
Yes, you were! But you came back to us when you thought Emily was dying. Oh, you deserve happiness!

CHARLOTTE
I shall write a note immediately and put it in the post. "To Whom It May Concern, Miss Charlotte Bronte deserves happiness and requests an affirmative response by the 5th, if possible." Will that do?

ANNE
Oh, but you do deserve happiness and you are writing at last to someone who appreciates you. Please read his letter again—please. As I am your dear, loving little sister to whom you can deny nothing. Let me share your love and joy, as I have none of my own.

CHARLOTTE
Hush, you shall have, you shall. Two spinsters in this family are quite enough.

ANNE
Sometimes I feel that I shall grow old and wither and die and never have someone to love and be loved.

CHARLOTTE
Hush now, your spirits are as changeable as this April weather. Come, drive away those rain clouds and we shall read our letter. Or better still, into the fire with it if it causes so much furor!

ANNE
All right—I promise I'll be still—only read me the letter.

CHARLOTTE
(SHE takes the letter out of the desk and begins to read.)
"My dear Miss Bronte. I can't tell you what these months have meant to me since I first read your poems and novels, especially the

one. I have waited for the post—hoping for another letter that is like an elixir from a strange and beautiful world—and now I intend to discover that dream world and the author who rules over it. May I have your permission to set out on my visit of exploration? Your humble servant, James Taylor."

ANNE
You are the girl of his dreams!

CHARLOTTE
But I don't really understand the letter at all. Emily's words are the ones that conjure up a dream world. Has he confused us as one? Or does he think I'm the Ellis Bell to whom he's written so often?

ANNE
Charlotte, why haven't you shown this letter to Emily?

CHARLOTTE
Emily has been so secretive these past months. We used to share all of our writing, but now she refuses to let me read her new novel. And she refuses to let me reveal our true identities. But I intend to tell Mr. Taylor the secret of our identity when he is here whether Emily will have it so or not.

(THE REV. MR. PATRICK BRONTE enters.)

MR. BRONTE
What is it? I heard you chattering away.

CHARLOTTE
Did we disturb you? I'm sorry. I think it is the spring sunshine that has touched our hearts.

MR. BRONTE
Where is Emily?

CHARLOTTE

I think she went out just after lunch.

MR. BRONTE

Really, Charlotte! You should not let her wander about in this changeable weather. You know she was quite ill this past winter with that abominable cough. I really feared consumption. You should not have let her go.

CHARLOTTE

You know that no one can stop Emily when she is determined to do something.

ANNE

(Crossing to the window and looking out.)
Oh, here comes Emily.

(The SOUND of a door OPENING is HEARD. EMILY BRONTE enters. SHE is carrying flowers, and HER cloak is trailing over one arm with HER hair falling about HER shoulders. Her moorlark, Psyche, is perched on her shoulder.)

EMILY

Oh, look! Look!
(SHE gives the flowers to Anne.)
They are all over the moors! I thought that I should die in the winter and the spring would forget me. But look, it has not forgotten! It has decked my kingdom for my return!

MR. BRONTE

Emily, you disobeyed me. You should not have gone out.

EMILY

Oh, please don't scold, Papa. The sun was warm on the hills, and I had to bring the warmth of spring into these shuttered rooms.

MR. BRONTE
The day looks warmer than it is—the wind is cold over the hills. You'll catch a chill.

ANNE
Oh, Emily, don't speak of dying. Your cheeks are glowing. You are so full of life.

(ANNE arranges the flowers in a bowl.)

EMILY
Oh, my dear Anne, my dear little mouse, nibbling away at the edges of life.

MR. BRONTE
Anne is right. There is a flush to your cheeks. I hope you're not feverish.

EMILY
Psyche, too, loved to be out on the moor. The open air has almost healed her broken wing.
(SHE opens the door of the cage, and puts Psyche inside. SHE whistles to the bird.)
Here, my pet, a sprig of heather to heal your wounded heart. Oh! The spring is so lovely!

CHARLOTTE
(Hugging EMILY.)
You are the spring, my sweet! It could not return if you were not here.

MR. BRONTE
Emily, I must forbid you to go out again until the weather is more certain. Your enthusiasm carries you away. You are never prudent.

EMILY
Then I am never prudent. All winter I have waited for the sound of the moorlark and the smell of the heather and the touch of the

wind over the moor. I feel that the world is all new and it is the first moment of creation. I have never seen it so lovely.

MR. BRONTE

Emily, you provoke me. I cannot get you to obey. You go your own way....

EMILY

Oh, I know dear papa, but I am so much better, really I am. You spoil me too much.

MR. BRONTE

You are my dear and beautiful spirit, and you know I could not bear to have you buffeted by the cruel winds of this world.

EMILY

This harsh winter is over and I am well again, and you find me dancing about the room like a feather ready to fly through the open window.

(SHE whirls him about.)

MR. BRONTE

Stop, stop, you silly girl! What would my parishioners say if they saw their minister whirling about the room in such a fashion?

ANNE

Oh, Papa, did you never dance at all?

MR. BRONTE

When I was young, but that was a long time ago. The young are foolish and have no thought for the morrow.

EMILY

You are never foolish, Papa—and all men should be foolish sometimes. But you are very dignified and very handsome. And when you go into Bradford, I can hear all of the whispers going 'round—

"There is the distinguished author of sermons, Patrick Bronte, who has the living at Haworth, and his three handsome daughters, who have artistic and literary leanings, I'm told."

MR. BRONTE
Yes, his three handsome daughters, who are the joy of his life, and his wastrel son, who will worry us all into our graves! He is only too well known.

ANNE
Papa, it is almost half past. You'll be late for your rounds.

MR. BRONTE
Please ask Jock to saddle my horse and bring the carriage.
    (To CHARLOTTE.)
I promised old Mrs. Lanham that you and Anne will visit with her today while I made my rounds.

CHARLOTTE
Oh, but Father, couldn't we go another day? There's so many chores I still have to do this afternoon.

MR. BRONTE
Charlotte! Am I to have no obedience in my own house? I shall expect you and Anne to join me at the carriage as soon as you get your cloaks.

CHARLOTTE and ANNE
Yes, Papa.

(CHARLOTTE and ANNE exit.)

MR. BRONTE
Where is Branwell? Did he go to his duties in the village or is he sulking about somewhere, waiting until I am gone, so that he can join his idle companions at the Black Bull.

EMILY
I saw him on the road to Bradford.

MR. BRONTE
More like the road to drink and damnation. Once I thought he had a touch of genius, but he has been nothing but a disappointment and a shame on this house. To have had his God-given talents and all come to naught. It is a sin to deny the gifts of God.

EMILY
Or only a sin if we deny what we are. If he is a trial to you, think what tortures he inflicts upon himself.

MR. BRONTE
Emily, you always defend him. Mark my words, one of these days I shall turn him out of the house to make his own way as I had to do before I was taken in by the good Rev. Tighe.

EMILY
The good Rev. Mr. Tighe didn't turn you out of doors.

MR. BRONTE
That he did not, for I was like a son to him. I didn't turn drunkard and wastrel to bite the hand that fed me.

EMILY
Perhaps Branwell is meeting your needs just as capably as you met Mr. Tighe's.

MR. BRONTE
Emily, this time you've gone too far! There are times when you are too outspoken and impertinent!

EMILY
(Striking a dramatic pose.)
Oh, forgive me, dear sir, or I shall throw myself into the flames and

you will never see me more. I shall commit suttee in the ancient and honorable tradition of India, and who will read to you then?

MR. BRONTE

No flames could consume your proud spirit. You would rise again like the phoenix out of the ashes.

EMILY

Ah, you do love me a little then and forgive my hasty tongue?

MR. BRONTE

You could charm the birds out of the trees and how can one old father's heart hold out against you.

(ANNE and CHARLOTTE enter wearing cloaks and bonnets.)

CHARLOTTE

Papa, it's almost half past.

MR. BRONTE

Emily, you should rest for a while. Anne and Charlotte will convey your regrets to Mrs. Lanham.

EMILY

(Mischievously glancing at Charlotte.)
Perhaps I am just a bit tired after all.

MR. BRONTE

You see, I was right. You have over exerted yourself. If I stop at the booksellers what shall I bring you?

EMILY

See if there is a new book of tales by Mr. Poe.

MR. BRONTE

That madman! His stories are not fit for the ears of young gentlewomen.

EMILY

But Father, we are not "young" gentlewomen. I do not think we are likely to be corrupted by a few tales by the mad genius, Mr. Poe.

MR. BRONTE

Genius? Disordered imagination!

EMILY

Now, Papa. Go on your rounds and bring me whatever you fancy from the booksellers. We shall read together tonight after dinner.

MR. BRONTE

Good day then. Anne and Charlotte, I shall have the carriage brought 'round. Do not keep me waiting.

CHARLOTTE

Yes, Father.

(HE exits.)

ANNE

Oh Charlotte, Mr. Taylor may come while we are gone!

EMILY

James Taylor? Our editor?

CHARLOTTE

Yes. He has written asking permission to come to Haworth today, and I have written to say that we should be happy to receive him. Do not be angry with me for not telling you, Emily. I thought you might say no. I should be here to receive him, but I dare not cross Father.

EMILY
Why not, Charlotte? We owe him our love and loyalty, but not our souls.

CHARLOTTE
You are the free spirit, Emily. You always have more courage than I would dare to have. I think that you would dare to cross God himself if he would not leave you free upon the moor.

EMILY
God is easier to cross than Father.

CHARLOTTE
Emily!

ANNE
Do hurry, Charlotte, or Father will be storming.

(SHE exits.)

EMILY
Charlotte, you should not have come back to Haworth. You were happy in Brussels—that was your freedom, but the moors are not for you.

CHARLOTTE
It is just that when I am alone on the moors, I feel that I am the last one left alive and all I have loved is gone and a chill goes through me.

EMILY
The moors will live when you and I are dead and gone.

CHARLOTTE
I must go. Promise you will not tell father of Mr. Taylor's visit—at least not yet. Will you promise?

EMILY

If you were wise you would not turn back to Haworth but would go as far as the horse's hoofs would carry you.

CHARLOTTE

Then I am not wise, but you said we should all be foolish sometimes. Goodbye, then, my dear, until tea.

> (CHARLOTTE exits. EMILY goes to the window and waves goodbye. SHE whistles to her lark. SHE goes to a sewing box in the corner and takes out a packet of letters. SHE lies down on the sofa with them on HER breast. LIGHTS DIM indicating the passing of time. After LIGHTS RISE, TABBY opens the door. SHE does not see EMILY.)

TABBY
> (Speaking to JAMES TAYLOR, who is OFF.)

Yes, sir, Miss Charlotte was expectin' you. Would you wait here in the sittin' room?

> (JAMES TAYLOR is ushered into the sitting room by TABBY.)

We don't receive visitors often at Haworth parsonage.

JAMES

It does seem to be a lonely spot.

TABBY

When I was a girl the pack-horses went through once a week with their tinkling bells and gay worsted. But when the railway came as far as Keighley there was no need for them. So Haworth is even quieter than it once was.

> (Pauses, looking out the window.)

Even the little people are gone.

JAMES

(Laughing.)
The little people?

TABBY

Do not laugh. I have known those who have seen the little people in the margin of the beck on moonlit nights. But that was when there were no mills in the valleys and all the wool-spinning was done by hand at home. It's the mills, I'm thinkin', have driven the little people away to the far moors. But even now it is not wise to laugh at the little people.

JAMES

If they are listening, I humbly ask them to forgive this thoughtless mortal.

TABBY

The little people have no time to spend on the silly doings of mortals.

(TABBY exits, closing the door. JAMES looks about the room without seeing EMILY on the sofa. Then HE turns to the window and looks out. HE whistles to the bird in the cage. EMILY gets up and stands in the shadows, looking at HIM. HE turns quickly and sees HER. HE is startled.)

JAMES

Ah! I'm sorry—you startled me. I did not hear you come in.

EMILY

But I did not come in. Perhaps I am the ghost of Haworth parsonage or a sprite from the moors.

JAMES

What happens to a moor sprite when she is discovered by a mortal?

EMILY

He must let her go or she dies.

JAMES

And if he should win her love, what would happen then?

EMILY

She must give up her kingdom and become only mortal. I know who you are. You are the Prince of the Kingdom of Light.

JAMES

Then I throw down my gauntlet to all comers.

EMILY

I must warn you that you have a terrible rival.

JAMES

And who is that?

EMILY

The Prince of the Kingdom of Shadows.

(There is a KNOCK at the door.)

TABBY
(Enters.)
I'm sorry, sir. I can't find Miss Charlotte—Oh....

JAMES

As you can see, Miss Bronte has found me.

EMILY

And the spell is broken and we are only mortals after all. It's all right, Tabby.

TABBY
Yes, Miss. Should I serve tea now?

EMILY
No. The others will join us later.
TABBY
Yes, Miss.

(SHE exits.)

JAMES
Am I exiled so soon?

EMILY
You must decide that for yourself. Perhaps Psyche will give you the answer.

JAMES
Psyche?

EMILY
(Crossing to the cage.)
My moorlark. I found her upon the moor in a storm and nursed her back to health. Now she follows me everywhere and comes when I call even though her wild wings long for the free sky. One day I shall have to let her go. But not now, not yet. I cannot bear to lose her yet. Sh-h-h....

(EMILY listens at the cage and then laughs.)

JAMES
And does she speak to you?

EMILY
She is telling me about you. Perhaps we are to be friends.

JAMES
I feel that through our letters we are already more than friends.

EMILY
Sometimes we deceive each other and ourselves without meaning to. Won't you sit down, Mr. Taylor?
(HE sits on the sofa.)
Mr. Taylor, let us understand one another. How—how can I explain? You see, you admire me as a poet and you have mistaken your admiration for—more than it is. I have saved all of your letters, your charming letters, your wonderful letters that made me laugh when I had not laughed in a long time and made me believe in hope when I thought there was no hope left in the world. I can't tell you how I have treasured your respect and understanding.

JAMES
My respect and admiration for the poet knows no bounds, but I wrote to the woman, Miss Bronte.

EMILY
Only the poet receives letters at Haworth Parsonage. Miss Bronte, the woman, went on a far journey long ago and has not returned.

JAMES
I must confess, that you are even more surprising than I imagined.

EMILY
Surprising?

JAMES
Yes, surprising and intriguing—that the passion and fire of *Wuthering Heights* could be conceived and nurtured in this out-of-the-way hamlet.

EMILY
Perhaps it seems out of the way to you. To me, it is the life I have always known.

JAMES
Have you never been away from here, then?

EMILY
When I was five, after my mother died, I was sent away to a school for the daughters of clergymen to teach us humility and self-denial.

JAMES
That is very young to be sent away. Were you very lonely?

EMILY
I had my two oldest sisters—until they became ill from the harsh and inhumane treatment, shut away from the moors and the freedom they loved. When I sickened and would have died, my father came and took us home. My sisters died soon after.

JAMES
Forgive me. I make you remember the sorrow you'd rather forget.

EMILY
No, I shall never forget. It was then I vowed that if I ever left there alive, I would never again do any man's bidding but only what I decided in my own heart. So here I am as you find me: a "surprising" product of this "out of the way hamlet." Now tell me about you, James Taylor.

JAMES
I, too, wanted to be a writer, but after Cambridge I had to find some means of making my way and so I became an editor. I've been with Smith and Elder for nearly ten years, and I think now I could not have made a wiser choice. My choice has led me here, to this lonely village and to the surprising author who lives here.

EMILY
And is London never lonely?

JAMES

It is the most alive city in the world. I couldn't begin to describe the true London. It is filthy and splendid, shameful and exciting, all at the same time. You would find much of my London both incredible and shocking.

EMILY

I'm not as innocent or as fragile as you imagine.

JAMES

There are daily events in London that make one ashamed of the human race. Children of nine labor fourteen hours a day, often chained at their tasks like animals. Children of both sexes are sold into prostitution, and destroyed by disease and drink. Women of the lower classes lie drunk in the gutter, their starving babes clutching at their breasts. The shrieks from the workhouses and madhouses set one's hair on end. Immense and thoughtless wealth exist side by side with grinding poverty. But just when I think I've grown to hate London for all her cruelty, she again reveals her fascination—and my God, the city is alive! Alive—breathing and warm and vital. You must let me show you London as I know her.

EMILY

I will never know London. But I know why you have come to Haworth.

JAMES

Do you?

EMILY

Yes. These mysterious authors have created something of a sensation and you want to be assured that you will handle their next novels. I can hear it now. "Of course I can be received by that strange recluse, Miss Bronte. What do you bet me that she invites me to tea and gives me the manuscripts after?" For one as young and handsome and persuasive as you, any lady is an easy mark and especially a spinster who is sometimes an invalid who writes poetry and who has never been loved before. They are the easiest of all.

JAMES

Is that what you believe?

EMILY

I can't believe anything else.

JAMES

Then why have you kept my letters by you as I have kept your letters to me? Do you remember what you said?

EMILY

No—I have forgotten.

JAMES

Then I'll remember for you. We need no letters now. You told me that the poet dares men to believe in the reality of wisdom and courage and love. And I know from your letters of the warmth and gentleness and love you have to give.

EMILY

My gentleness is only resignation, and my courage—desperation, and my warmth—my warmth is the last flame of a fever that saps my life. I have nothing to give—nothing.

JAMES

Then you are not the woman who wrote those letters. If these letters trap us in lies then we shall consign them to their own hell and go our way alone. Into the cleansing flames then!

(HE starts to throw the letters into the fire.)

EMILY
(Frenziedly trying to grab the letters from HIM.)
You shall not. They are my letters—mine! They came in this last desperate winter when I had almost despaired—had almost given up. Do you know how easy it is to die when you are very ill? You have only to decide that you cannot fight anymore and then open your hand and let the golden sunbeams spill upon the floor leaving only the shadow. Your letters came when I thought I had nothing else to live for, and you drew me back into life. If you destroy those letters now, then take my life with them!

JAMES
Your life is in my hands then. You have given it to me and I shall never let you go.

>(THEY both clutch the letters in an intense moment that is on the edge of an embrace when THEY hear voices outside.)

TABBY
(Outside the door, OFF.)
Yes, he's come. Your visitor is in the sitting room with Miss Emily.

EMILY
It's Charlotte and Anne.

JAMES
(Puzzled. Releases letters.)
Charlotte and Anne?

EMILY
Yes, my sisters.

JAMES
But I thought there was only one Miss Bronte.

EMILY

There are three of us.

JAMES

Then you are...?

EMILY

I am Emily Bronte.
>(CHARLOTTE, ANNE, and TABBY enter. CHARLOTTE and ANNE remove their bonnets and cloaks.)

CHARLOTTE

Mr. Taylor, I'm so sorry we weren't here to greet you. I know you must think us inexcusably rude.

JAMES

Not at all...Miss Bronte, I trust?

CHARLOTTE

Yes, Charlotte Bronte. I see that you and Emily have met already.

JAMES

Ah—yes.

CHARLOTTE

This is our youngest sister Anne.

JAMES

Your servant, ma'am.

TABBY

Shall I bring tea, Miss?

CHARLOTTE

Thank you, Tabby.

(TABBY exits.)

CHARLOTTE

I've so looked forward to meeting you in person, Mr. Taylor. I could almost believe that Smith, Elder, and Co. were a fiction, a product of my wishful imagination.

JAMES

And we believed you were a fiction, those mysterious brothers Currer, Ellis, and Acton Bell.

CHARLOTTE

But you see we are not mysterious, nor are we brothers.

JAMES

And so the mystery is even more intriguing.

CHARLOTTE

It seemed the only way we could have our work published was to go disguised as male authors. I had to persuade Emily to submit her work, and then only if we concealed our real identities.

JAMES

And what was your reason, Miss Anne?

ANNE

It seemed great fun to go in disguise. We have always created our own world and enacted the characters of our creation.

JAMES

All of literary England is awaiting your next novels and Smith, Elder, and Co. would be honored to be your publisher. Are your next works already in progress?

CHARLOTTE

Anne and I have almost completed our new novels, but you will have to ask Emily about her novel. She has been very mysterious about this one and will let no one see it.

JAMES
I hope you will let me share your mystery, Miss Emily.

EMILY
Perhaps there is no mystery, Mr. Taylor. Perhaps there is only the simple world contained within these four walls.

JAMES
For one who has the heart to look, that is mystery enough for a lifetime.

ANNE
You must persuade her, Mr. Taylor.

JAMES
I shall, Miss Anne.

TABBY
(Entering with the tea things.)
Here's your tea. Now pour it while it's hot. Mr. Taylor has been waiting long enough.

ANNE
Oh, Tabby! You've made scones.

CHARLOTTE
There's nothing like Tabby's scones in all of England.

TABBY
You and your flattering tongue. Mr. Taylor is from London and will have had very grand scones indeed compared to these poor Yorkshire ones.

JAMES
If yours taste half as good as they look, I may never be persuaded to return to London.

ANNE
Please take one bite now, Mr. Taylor, or Tabby will die of anticipation.

JAMES
(HE takes one of the scones and bites into it.)
Ah—ah—Tabby! Has anyone yet asked for your hand? A lass who bakes scones like this should be wed tomorrow.

TABBY
Tomorrow is it? I'll put on me bonnet this very afternoon!

(TABBY exits. CHARLOTTE pours tea and offers sugar and cream.)

JAMES
We understand in London that there is a Bronte brother. Coming from such a family he must be equally talented. I look forward to meeting him.

ANNE
He is talented in so many ways. He can draw and write and paint. He can create a speaking likeness you would not believe.

CHARLOTTE
Branwell has not been well and has been—unable to attempt authorship for publication.

JAMES
I'm sorry, I did not realize he had been so ill.

EMILY
Not ill, Mr. Taylor. Only dying slowly by his own hand.

CHARLOTTE
Emily!
   (To JAMES.)
It is only Emily's odd—jest. Branwell is not dying.

   (BRANWELL BRONTE appears outside the open window.)

EMILY
You are right, Charlotte. The Branwell we once knew is already dead.

BRANWELL
Dead? Indeed? I assure you that I am one of the most alive dead men you'll ever meet! My sister must learn to distinguish between her wishes and reality.

EMILY
I don't wish you dead, Branwell.

BRANWELL
I take a wish for my death as a kindly wish and thank you for it.
   (HE jumps into the room from the window.)

CHARLOTTE
Oh, Branwell, I thought you had gone early to Bradford. I told father....

BRANWELL
I know what you told father: "The prodigal son has gone off to work like a man." But you see, Charlotte, there is no work to go off to.

CHARLOTTE
Oh, Branwell, you didn't...?

BRANWELL

Yes, correct as usual, Charlotte. I was relieved of my position yesterday morning.

CHARLOTTE

Oh, no, Branwell, what will father say?

BRANWELL

Oh, yes, Charlotte, and you know what father will say.

ANNE

But you left the house. I saw you go.

BRANWELL

I rested comfortably behind a tombstone until father's horse was safely over the hill. So Emily's right—as usual. I have risen from the dead.
    (HE is pretending to be drunker than HE actually
    is.)
But who is this? You are all fluttering about him like sparrows! How did Charlotte find you? There are so few eligible men in the village. She must have sent a letter to God. It is so like her.

CHARLOTTE

Branwell! You must mind your manners. This is Mr. Taylor from our publishing firm, Smith, Elder, and Co. This is our brother—Branwell.

    (JAMES offers to shake hands, but BRANWELL
    grandly turns aside.)

BRANWELL

Our publishing firm, of course! Our publishing firm!

CHARLOTTE

Yes. Mr. Taylor has come all the way from London. Let me pour you a cup of hot tea.

BRANWELL
Do you really think I need anything more to drink, Charlotte? Then this will do nicely.
> (HE takes a flask from his coat pocket and takes a swig.)

Busy, busy Charlotte. You think you have only to try hard enough and all will come right in the end. What you don't understand, my dear, is that for all your trying, it won't come right in the end.
> (Speaking cynically to JAMES.)

You must forgive us, Mr. Taylor, for out boorishness. We are children of a country parson unaccustomed to the polite society and sophistications of London. Instead, we are surrounded by thoughts of hell-fire and damnation and of the briefness of this earthly life. You see, Mr. Taylor, this is Charlotte's damnation. She believes that if we only try hard enough it will all come right in the end. What she doesn't realize is that it is not the end that matters—only the endeavor. We must choose that or nothing. And I choose nothing.

CHARLOTTE
Branwell, you are being unspeakably rude to Mr. Taylor.

BRANWELL
No, Charlotte. I am speaking as plainly as I can. I want our publisher to understand why he has never published anything of mine.
> (BRANWELL stands before JAMES like a cocky thief before a judge.)

It is because, Mr. Taylor, I disdain the petty, mean, vicious, dismal world that exists, the only world we have to endeavor in if we choose to endeavor at all.

ANNE
Oh, Branwell, please....

BRANWELL
Ah, my sweet Anne, my angelic Anne. And what is your damnation, my love? Yours is the worst of all, I think. For your "nothing"

is that nothing will ever happen to you. You will never love or hate or have children or grow old. You will never know the sweetness of temptation or the enticements of remorse. You will only die, my sweet Anne, and be buried with your untried chastity.

ANNE

Oh, Branwell, we love you....

BRANWELL

Yes, I know, but that is not enough. That is never enough. And what are your words to the prodigal, Emily?

EMILY

Only what you already know. You think to ease your own suffering by inflicting pain on others, but you only turn the knife deeper in your own wound. You have chosen the illusion of renunciation and so have lost the dream.

BRANWELL

At least I know my illusions—my alcohol and my opium. They replace this bleak moor with a world more bearable and remote. But what of your dreams, my wise Emily, my courageous Emily? What is your damnation? It is just as mine. You can no more live in this world than can I. You try to fly with your poor fragile wings against the sun, only realizing when it is too late and the wax is already melting between your feathers that you are only human after all and were never meant for the upper air. Forget your dreams and taste my opium, Emily.

>   (HE takes a small bottle out of his pocket and roughly puts it to her lips.)

It is an easier death than that long, sickening plunge when the cold earth rushes up to meet you.

>   (EMILY, unable to bear any more, rushes out of the room.)

It's the truth that hurts the most, isn't it, Emily?

CHARLOTTE
Branwell!

BRANWELL
My dear Charlotte, wouldn't you be disappointed if I didn't play my accustomed role of the fallen genius?
    (Turning to JAMES.)
And what is your opinion of the merry games we Brontes play, Mr. Taylor?

JAMES
I will express my opinion at another time and place.

TABBY
    (Entering.)
What has gotten into Miss Emily? She went out past me as if the devil himself were after her.
    (Sees BRANWELL.)
Oh, I see. It is the devil. Why aren't you at your work in the village?

BRANWELL
Why would the devil be content to work in a mere village when he has so much more scope in the bosom of his family?

CHARLOTTE
We must go after her! Father will never forgive us if she becomes ill again.

BRANWELL
Father is long past forgiving me, and besides, I don't feel up to acts of heroism today.

TABBY
Nor have you for some time.

CHARLOTTE

Oh, Branwell, you don't mean what you say, you and Emily. It is some childish game. Go after her.

BRANWELL

Oh, but you are wrong, Charlotte. We are no longer children. It is a game that is in earnest, and she can go to Hell for all of me.

(BRANWELL quickly exits.)

CHARLOTTE

Anne, go after him. Don't let him leave the house. I must talk to him before Father returns. Tabby, if you should hear Father's horse on the road, please let me know immediately.
(ANNE and TABBY exit.)
Oh, Mr. Taylor, what you must think of us? Please find Emily bring her back. She has a reckless courage that never admits of danger until it is too late. Even as a child she would venture where Branwell and I would never dare to follow. And she has been so strange this past winter. I hardly know her anymore. Please, Mr. Taylor. I already value your friendship. Go after her.

JAMES

Which way would she go?

CHARLOTTE

She'll be on the path to Blackstone Edge. Go round past the stable and up the hill. You'll see a path there.

JAMES

Don't worry. I'll find her. She'll be all right.

(JAMES exits. CHARLOTTE crosses to the window and looks out. When SHE hears BRANWELL at the door, SHE turns to him. BRANWELL enters and throws HIMSELF on the sofa before the fire.)

BRANWELL
Well, Charlotte, what is the text of your next sermon for today? My drinking or my deplorable behavior?

CHARLOTTE
I want to know the truth. Why were you dismissed as clerk at Manchester and Leeds?

BRANWELL
What does it matter now? They won't take me back, so don't go to them.

CHARLOTTE
Your sisters are counting on you. How else are we to survive? What are our choices? Marriage? To my knowledge no one has asked. Should we become governesses? You've seen to what disaster that's led. You have all the choices, Branwell, and you've squandered them all, and our futures as well!

BRANWELL
It seems you and Emily have done all right without me.

CHARLOTTE
Tell me. Why did you lose your position as tutor at Thorpe Green? I thought the Robinsons were very well pleased with you conduct. But when I went to see Mr. Robinson, he would not even discuss the reasons for your dismissal, and he even refused to give you a recommendation.

BRANWELL
You should not have gone to Thorpe Green! It was none of your business!

CHARLOTTE
Was it the drinking? Tell me honestly.

BRANWELL
No, it was not the drinking. I made an effort to be what they wanted—the proper English gentleman.

CHARLOTTE
Then I don't understand. When you first took the position, Mrs. Robinson said she valued you highly. She told me once how very pleased she was with your services.

BRANWELL
Oh, yes, she valued me highly and was, indeed, very pleased with my services. She told me that same thing many times.

CHARLOTTE
Speak plainly. Your words mean more than they say.

BRANWELL
Just as I said, Charlotte. She valued me highly and was, indeed, very pleased with my services. Surely you understand. You are an intelligent woman—a published author—who knows about life and love.

CHARLOTTE
What are you saying?

BRANWELL
If you don't know what I am saying, how can you write about men and women? If your heroes and heroines don't have any blood in their veins, what are they, puppet figures playing at life and death?

CHARLOTTE
Branwell, do you mean that...

BRANWELL
I mean, Charlotte, to put it plainly, that I was her lover. During the day I instructed her children in history and philosophy, but at night

she instructed me in the art of love. And she did, indeed, value my services—although her husband, when he began to suspect us, did not.

CHARLOTTE

Oh, Branwell, how could you? You were in a position of trust! How could you?

BRANWELL

If you don't know that there can be something dark between a man and a woman that is beyond petty morality, beyond age and time—when for that moment the only reality is the rhythm of two pulses throbbing as one—if you don't know that, then I can't tell you.

CHARLOTTE

You would throw everything away for a wild moment. And now that moment is gone and everything with it.

BRANWELL

That wild moment is everything to me. I would throw away the whole world to have her in my bed again. Instead, we steal a brief hour once in a fortnight and she is gone before my fingertips have again learned her touch. And each time she leaves me more feverish than before.

CHARLOTTE

Oh, Branwell, let her go! She'll destroy you and herself. What if her husband should verify his suspicions?

BRANWELL

Then maybe she'll go away with me as I've wanted her to.

CHARLOTTE

Oh, Branwell, no! Think of the scandal. It would ruin father in the district.

BRANWELL

Father be damned!

CHARLOTTE

If you won't think of Father or your sisters, think of yourself. How would you live? You have no money and no position.

BRANWELL

But she will have both money and position when her husband dies which I hope will be very soon. When his heart gives out, we intend to make the most of all the money he's hoarded.

CHARLOTTE

Branwell!

(A SOUND of a HORSE'S hooves is heard OFF.)

ANNE

(Entering.)
Charlotte, Father is coming up the road.

CHARLOTTE

(To Branwell.)
He must not see you like this. Go out through the kitchen—now hurry.

(BRANWELL hurriedly exits.)

ANNE

Oh, Charlotte, what are we to do? What are we to do?

CHARLOTTE

I don't know, Anne. I don't know. But Branwell was wrong about one thing. I don't think it will all come right in the end.

END ACT I: SCENE ONE

ACT I: SCENE TWO

(The moor near Haworth. A crag of rocks rises sharply at stage left and upstage. It is mid-afternoon the same day. EMILY is alone, sheltered by the high rocks behind HER.)

EMILY

I fear the tide of grief must flow
Undaunted down the years.
But where is all my anguish now?
Where are all my tears?

JAMES

(Enters.)

Miss Emily.

EMILY

Emily is not here. She is down there at Haworth parsonage, sitting before the fire, drinking tea. This is my kingdom.

JAMES

And do I have permission to enter your kingdom?

EMILY

Yes. I want you to see how beautiful it is.

(HE climbs up to HER and stands, looking all about at the moors.)

Look, all the drabness of Haworth becomes enchantment at this distance. And see the clouds that pass over the moor and how they darken the heather in their passing. They are great ships from a strange land laden with colored silks and white sea pearls. Look now, how the heather changes from gold to violet and deep purple. See—just there—a doe and her fawn.

JAMES

Where? I can't see.

EMILY

Just off there, near those grey rocks. She is very still. Now, did you see the flick of her tail? She's bounding off and her fawn behind her.

JAMES

Yes, I see her now.

EMILY

When she has no fawns with her, she has come and eaten from my hand. Her nose is softer than wood moss, and her eyes are big and gentle, as if she could almost speak.

JAMES

The moors have a stark beauty.

EMILY

Don't let their beauty deceive you. They can be as cruel as they are beautiful. When winter comes and the storm clouds gather dark and fierce over Blackstone Edge, not many dare venture out to test that cruelty. Then the wind tears about the house on winter nights like a wild beast seeking entrance. And there are sometimes sudden blasts that sweep down from the north and freeze the sheep where they stand and the shepherds with them.
  (Pause.)
But in spring, it is a land of enchantment and wild beauty.

JAMES

I think you love it very much.

EMILY

I feel that if some great wind swept over these moors destroying every bush and valley and hill, I could create it all again out of my own heart—leaf by leaf and rock by rock.

(THEY gaze at the moor for a moment.)

JAMES
I'm afraid it was my presence that provoked your brother to that outburst.

EMILY
No, his own despair and torment are enough. If you only knew him as he was. Not the bitter and desperate creature he is now, but the fierce, proud boy he once was. Now you see only a driven creature that, like a mad dog, snaps and snarls at whoever comes near him.

JAMES
How have you and your sisters managed to endure such treatment?

EMILY
He is our brother.

JAMES
Your sisters love you very much.

EMILY
Anne is as you see her. Never complaining—never a word for herself. And Charlotte always makes plans for all of us. Once she tried to set up a school for young ladies. We sent out our brochure and opened our doors. There was only one problem—no one came—no one at all. It was really very funny.
(Pause.)
Poor Charlotte. She doesn't belong here. She almost escaped once. She got as far as Brussels as a teacher in a girl's school. Then I came down with a wretched fever and Father wrote her of it and she came home. I was furious with her and swore never to speak to her again if she did not return at once to Brussels. But she would not leave and instead cared for me morning, noon, and night until I had to speak just to get her to leave me alone.

JAMES

Your sisters are devoted to you.

EMILY

They are fools, fools! What good will their love and devotion do if it destroys them? I want their happiness not their devotion. Sometimes I feel that I am the center of a whirlpool that revolves 'round and 'round me and when I go down they will all go down with me.
    (Pause.)
That's why I have to get away here, where there is no love or devotion, no yesterday or tomorrow—only now. These moors and hills—this is where I am free.

JAMES

All of this seems very serene.

EMILY

Not serene. Nothing so romantic as serene. Only unspeaking, unknowing, uncaring, always, and forever. If all human eyes should watch and weep, the moor would not return a single sigh.
    (Pause.)
This is not your world, James Taylor. Go back to your London. That is where you belong.

JAMES

You're shivering. The wind has turned cold.

EMILY

When the sun goes down behind Blackstone Edge, there is a chill in the air.

JAMES

Here, take my coat.
    (HE takes off HIS coat and tenderly puts it around HER shoulders.)
Is that better?

EMILY

Yes—I think you are able to live in your London, James Taylor, because you believe it exists.

JAMES

I want you to believe it—to know it—as I do. It is real.

EMILY

Is it? I do believe in one thing.

JAMES

What is that?

EMILY

That today has been one of the happiest days of my life.

JAMES

And one of the happiest of mine.

EMILY

And that is a lot to believe in. I never thought I should have so much.

JAMES

Emily—I want to....

EMILY

Sh-h-h! We mustn't break the spell of this moment. I must go back now. The sun is going down. That is the road to Haworth Village. It will be quicker for you if you take that way.

JAMES

I'll go back to the house with you.

EMILY

I could find my way on a moonless night and without the stars, but tonight there will be stars. See? The first evening stars are already softening the twilight.

(SHE hands HIM his coat.)

JAMES

No, keep it until tomorrow. As I walk back to the inn, I'll think of you in my coat, warmed and sheltered from the wind.

(HE slowly exits.)

ANNE

(Entering.)

Emily! Emily!

EMILY

I'm here.

ANNE

Charlotte sent me to find you. Father is home. He'll be furious if he learns you've been out a second time today.
(EMILY stands for a long moment.)
What are you thinking, Emily? You—you frighten me when you look like that.

EMILY

How do I look?

ANNE

You look—as if you had gone away and might not come back again. What are you thinking when you look like that?

EMILY

I am thinking how far away London is.

ANNE

Let's go down to the house. The wind is getting cold. Aren't you coming?

EMILY

Yes, go on. I'll follow.
            (ANNE exits.)
Spring retreats and from its fate
My fate cannot be severed.
But this one day of happiness
Is in my heart forever.
This one day of happiness
Is in my heart forever.

END ACT I: SCENE TWO

ACT I: SCENE THREE

(Early afternoon, the next day. The sitting room of the Bronte house.)

TABBY
(Entering.)
Miss Charlotte, your father's curate, Mr. Nicholls is waiting in the hall. He came in at the kitchen with his hat in his hand like a scared rabbit afraid that the hounds would catch his scent. I think if I had said boo to him he would have turned tail and fled.

CHARLOTTE
(Laughing.)
Oh, Tabby, you are unkind to poor Mr. Nicholls. He is so well-meaning.

TABBY
He's well-meaning but he does preach a dull sermon. There's not a living spark of brimstone or hell-fire in it.

CHARLOTTE
Did you tell him that father is in the study?

TABBY
I did, but he asked to see Mr. Bronte in the sitting room. And he asked especially if you were at home. "Is Miss Charlotte at home," says he. "And do you want to see her?" says I. "Oh, no!" says he. "But would Mr. Bronte do me the honor of seeing me in the sitting room?" says he.

CHARLOTTE
He asked about me? We've hardly spoken two words together in the two years he's been here. Well, don't keep the poor man waiting. Do send him in and we'll see if we can't persuade him to go into father's study. But I do hope Mr. Nicholls won't make Father late for his rounds.

TABBY

Mr. Bronte said particularly that he must start promptly at half past.

CHARLOTTE

Remember our secret. Have you forgotten that Mr. Taylor is coming again today for tea?

TABBY

Forget, indeed! I've fixed Mr. Taylor cakes and nut bread the like of which he'll never find in London.

CHARLOTTE

I think he's won your heart, Tabby.

TABBY

If he's won a heart, it's a younger one that mine, I'm thinkin'.
    (SHE exits. OFF.)
Miss Charlotte asked that you step into the sitting room.

NICHOLLS

    (OFF.)
Oh, yes—yes—thank you, Tabby.
    (HE is HEARD to stumble against the hall table.)
Oh, I'm so sorry! I do hope it isn't scratched.

TABBY

It's all right, sir. Curates come and go, but the furniture stays forever. Go right on in.

(NICHOLLS enters nervously.)

CHARLOTTE

Mr. Nicholls, do come in. Father's busy with his sermon. I'll just let him know you're here.

NICHOLLS
Yes—I mean, no—thank you. I think it would be best—that is, more appropriate if I see him in the sitting room—thank you—if you don't mind.

TABBY
Mr. Bronte doesn't take to a disturbin' of his routine. He'll be some put out.

NICHOLLS
Yes, I know, and I hate to disturb him, but I thought—well, the nature of my business—not exactly business, you understand—a personal matter—you see, Miss Charlotte. It's—it's rather overpowering to confront both Mr. Bronte and his study at once.

CHARLOTTE
I'll tell him that you're here then, and leave you two alone. Come, Tabby. Good afternoon, Mr. Nicholls. I hope that the—business you've come about turns out well for you.

NICHOLLS
Oh, thank you, Miss Charlotte. Thank you with all my heart.

> (NICHOLLS looks around nervously. Finally building up HIS courage, HE sits down on the edge of the sofa. Just at that moment the door opens and MR. BRONTE enters. NICHOLLS jumps up immediately in confusion.)

MR. BRONTE
Well, Nicholls, Tabby says you want to see me. I was going to send for you. If my sight is as bleary as it has been this week past, you may have to stand in for me in the pulpit.

NICHOLLS
Whatever I can do to assist you, sir.

MR. BRONTE
I know I can count on you, Nicholls. You're the most reliable curate I've ever had. These eyes are a confounded nuisance, but then it's God's will and must be endured. Has old Rankin come up with an estimate on the charges for repairs to the west wing of the church? He drives a sharp bargain, so be prepared to offer him half of what he demands.

NICHOLLS
I haven't come on church business.

MR. BRONTE
Not on church business?

NICHOLLS
It's a matter of a personal nature, sir, and—well, a matter of some delicacy.

MR. BRONTE
Well, come to the point, man.

NICHOLLS
It is a matter that I have thought about carefully for some months now. In fact I might say, have thought about almost from the moment I arrived at Haworth Village, over two years ago last month. So I hope you will not think it is a hasty decision or one that has been arrived at without due thought and judgment.

MR. BRONTE
Yes, Nicholls, I know you are one who thinks long and carefully before you speak. In fact, now that we're on that subject, your sermon of a month ago Sunday last was—well, that's another matter—what was it you came to see me about? I'll have to start my parish rounds within the next half hour.

NICHOLLS

Well, sir, as a matter of fact—sir, I have the honor to ask your permission to pay my respects to your eldest daughter and ask for her hand in marriage.

MR. BRONTE

You have the honor to—what?

NICHOLLS

To—ah—to ask your permission—ah—to pay my respects to your eldest daughter and ask for her hand in marriage.

MR. BRONTE

Marriage? My eldest daughter?

NICHOLLS

Yes, sir.

MR. BRONTE

Do you mean Charlotte?

NICHOLLS

Yes, sir, Miss Charlotte, whom I hold in the highest honor and esteem.

MR. BRONTE

Have you spoken to Charlotte of this?

NICHOLLS

Not yet, sir, I wanted to get your permission first.

MR. BRONTE

I see. Mr. Nicholls, I have valued your dedication as my curate. I should, therefore, hate to lose your services. I am, however, a man who speaks plainly and bluntly, as you know. Charlotte is of age. I cannot, therefore, absolutely forbid you to speak to her.

(After a long pause.)
In my own youth I entered into the bond of marriage, for I feared the depth of sin in my own heart and the depravity to which I might be tempted without the shield of marriage. But I cannot countenance the institution of marriage for my own daughters, knowing that it is founded on the sins and weakness of the flesh. I fear that physically my daughters are too delicate to endure the strains of marriage and childbirth. You must know, Mr. Nicholls, that there is a tendency to consumption and an early death in my wife's family. She, herself, succumbed to that disease—as did our two oldest children. In this fallen world, Mr. Nicholls, it is a stern God who tests our faith.

NICHOLLS
Amen, to that, Sir.

MR. BRONTE
Mr. Nicholls, I shall forget that you came to me this afternoon, for I would not wish that this visit should be a source of embarrassment to either you or myself.

NICHOLLS
I am sorry, sir. I, too, must speak plainly. Unless you absolutely forbid it, I must ask Miss Charlotte herself to give me her answer. And because I realize this will be a source of embarrassment to you, I'll send my resignation tomorrow morning. I'll, of course, stay until you find a replacement.

MR. BRONTE
If you feel you must go I will, of course, write you a letter of recommendation. I shall hate to lose your services.

NICHOLLS
Thank you, sir.

MR. BRONTE
I'll be late for my rounds. I'll wish you good day.

(MR. BRONTE exits. NICHOLLS begins to pace nervously.)

CHARLOTTE
(Entering.)
From the frown on his face I think your business with Father did not prosper.

NICHOLLS
No, I'm afraid he did not approve. If—you could spare me a moment, Miss Charlotte, there's something I want to discuss with you. May I sit down?

CHARLOTTE
Well—of course.

NICHOLLS
Thank you.
(HE sits on the sofa by the fire and lapses into an embarrassed silence.)

CHARLOTTE
(CHARLOTTE sits opposite HIM finally breaks the silence.)
Your duties as curate seem to keep you very busy. I know Father treasures your help.

NICHOLLS
I felt it an honor that your father chose me as his curate. His sermons are admired throughout the district for their vigor and power. I might even say greatly admired.

CHARLOTTE
Thank you. I'm sure that he's indebted to you for coming to such an out-of-the-way place as Haworth.

NICHOLLS
It is I who am indebted to him. I've valued the associations and the acquaintances that I have made here.

CHARLOTTE
Was there—ah—something in particular you wanted to see me about, Mr. Nicholls?

NICHOLLS
Oh—oh—yes. I had heard in the village, Miss Bronte, that you had a visitor from London. They say that he is from a firm that publishes books.

CHARLOTTE
Yes. My sisters and I have written poems and novels under—under assumed masculine names—and our work is being published in London by Mr. Taylor's firm

NICHOLLS
I see.

CHARLOTTE
But I had expected you to be surprised—about our writing, I mean.

NICHOLLS
Oh, no. Writing poems or novels need not be any less praiseworthy a pastime for young ladies than needlework or embroidery?

CHARLOTTE
I suppose that is a charitable way to see the matter.

NICHOLLS
You and your sisters all have lively imaginations. I feel quite dull beside you.

CHARLOTTE
Oh, no! You are too modest.

NICHOLLS
I am quite award of my limitations. They are God's will, and I am content with them.

CHARLOTTE
What can I say to that?

NICHOLLS
My present concern is with this London publisher and his visit to Haworth.

CHARLOTTE
But why should you be concerned about Mr. Taylor's visit?

NICHOLLS
He may intend to take you away.

CHARLOTTE
Take me away? I don't understand.

NICHOLLS
Miss Charlotte, that broth you sent last winter when I was ill—and the muffler you knitted for my Christmas present—I've treasured that muffler.

CHARLOTTE
Why, thank you, Mr. Nicholls. But the muffler must not have been thick enough, for it didn't keep you from getting a chill and being quite sick indeed.

NICHOLLS

Oh, no, Miss Charlotte, it wasn't the fault of the muffler. You see, I went out late one afternoon and forgot it. I'm afraid I'm rather forgetful. But I have treasured it.

CHARLOTTE

Even if you forget to wear it?

NICHOLLS

Oh, Miss Bronte, I treasure it above anything I own.

CHARLOTTE

Why, thank you, Mr. Nicholls. Then next Christmas I shall knit you some gloves to match—so that you may forget them, too, along with the forgotten muffler.

NICHOLLS

You're making fun of me, and I deserve it. I may forget the muffler when I go out, but I assure you, Miss Bronte, I never forget the kind hand that knitted it.

CHARLOTTE

I am expecting Mr. Taylor shortly, for tea. You were saying....

NICHOLLS

I—ah—Mr. Taylor is coming for tea? Well....
    (Suddenly determined.)
Yes, thank you, I—I will stay for tea.

CHARLOTTE

    (Surprised.)
Oh? Yes—well, I'll just tell Tabby there will be one more for tea. If you'll excuse me.
    (SHE exits. There is a KNOCK at the front door, OFF, then the sound of the door OPENING.)

CHARLOTTE
(OFF.)
I'm so glad you could join us, Mr. Taylor. Please do come into the sitting room.
(CHARLOTTE and JAMES enter.)
This is Mr. Arthur Nicholls, my father's curate—Mr. James Taylor, our publisher. Won't you both sit down? I must tell Tabby that we'll have tea shortly.

(CHARLOTTE exits hurriedly. There is an awkward silence between the TWO MEN.)

JAMES
You are Mr. Bronte's curate, Mr.—ah—Nicholls?

NICHOLLS
I've been assisting Mr. Bronte the past two years. His eyes have been troubling him—cataracts, I believe—and he asked me to take on the duties as curate.

JAMES
I see.

NICHOLLS
You are—from London—I believe?

JAMES
Yes.

NICHOLLS
I cannot imagine a decent sort of life in a city of 150,000 with the houses piled on top of one another.

JAMES
One grows used to it.

(There is another awkward silence.)

NICHOLLS

Look here—do you—do you mean to persuade Miss Bronte to go to London?

JAMES

Is that any business of yours, Mr. Nicholls?

NICHOLLS

It isn't my business at all, I suppose, but, yes it is! I feel that Miss Bronte should not make such a decision without a friend to rely upon and I intend to stand in the place of a friend—if she will have me.

JAMES

I, too, intend to be a friend on whom Miss Bronte can rely, Mr. Nicholls.

CHARLOTTE

(Entering.)

The tea will be here shortly. Anne will join us in a moment. I'm afraid I can't find Emily anywhere. I seem to be always apologizing to you, Mr. Taylor. I know you came to Haworth with the express purpose of discussing the publications of our next novels; and we don't seem to be making any progress in that direction. So far you must feel your trip from London has been a waste.

JAMES

Miss Charlotte, believe me, this trip has been more important to me than I ever dreamed possible.

NICHOLLS

Do you intend to return to London soon, Mr. Taylor?

JAMES
Not until I've completed my mission to Haworth, Mr. Nicholls.
(To CHARLOTTE.)
Will Miss Emily be joining us soon, do you think?

CHARLOTTE
Emily is so unpredictable. I hope you will forgive her. She goes her own way and is—different from anyone else. Once she saw a stray dog in the stable yard. When she tried to give it food and water, it suddenly turned and lunged at her. Its teeth ripped her arm, and it ran off to the moor to die, foaming at the mouth. Emily went into the kitchen and took up the poker and thrust it into the coals until it was white hot, and then held it on the wound in her arm. She never told anyone until she knew that the weeks of danger were over and that she would not go mad. I should not have had that courage, Mr. Taylor. She is the most unusual person I have ever known.

JAMES
Then we agree, Miss Charlotte. For I, too, think she is the most unusual person I have ever known.

ANNE
(Entering.)
Am I late? Forgive me.

NICHOLLS
Please, take my seat, Miss Anne.

ANNE
No, don't get up, Mr. Nicholls. I'll just sit here on the foot stool.

JAMES
Do join us. I've seen so little of you.

ANNE
I keep very busy.

(While THEY are ALL sitting down, TABBY opens the door and enters with the tea.)

TABBY
Here's your tea and an extra cup for Mr. Nicholls.

CHARLOTTE
Please put it here, Tabby.

NICHOLLS
(Making a place for HIMSELF nearer CHARLOTTE and sitting.)
I'll just—sit here.

CHARLOTTE
Why—yes, of course.

ANNE
What do you think of Haworth, Mr. Taylor?

JAMES
It is charming but a bit isolated. Your novellas are already famous in London, Miss Anne. You and your sisters must come and allow London Society to lionize you.

ANNE
To London? Oh, Charlotte!

CHARLOTTE
London!

NICHOLLS
I should think that God-fearing young ladies would do well to stand apart from London society. I shouldn't want my daughter to....

JAMES
Oh, you have a daughter?

NICHOLLS
Sir! I am unmarried, although I do not intend so to remain.

JAMES
Then you have a fiancée?

NICHOLLS
Not—ah –yet.

JAMES
But you have plans.

NICHOLLS
Yes, I have plans.

JAMES
Then good wishes to you.
    (Turning to ANNE and CHARLOTTE.)
Now as to your trip to London…

NICHOLLS
But my plans involve no trip to London.

JAMES
Sir, I had not known that I'd invited you.

NICHOLLS
If you have come to Haworth for the purpose of inducing Miss Charlotte Bronte to marry you and move to London, then I must oppose such a purpose with all my heart and soul!

CHARLOTTE

Mr. Nicholls!

JAMES

Marry Miss Charlotte? Induce her to move to London? Sir, are you mad?
    (To CHARLOTTE.)
Ma'am, you are a lovely and most marriageable young lady, but I....

CHARLOTTE

Please, Mr. Taylor, I quite understand.
    (Torn between confusion, anger, and pity.)
Mr. Nicholls! I simply don't know what has possessed you!
    (Calling into the other room.)
Tabby! Tabby! Will you bring Mr. Nicholls his hat?

NICHOLLS

Miss Charlotte, how can you ever forgive me?

ANNE
    (To NICHOLLS, comfortingly.)
I think it is best that you go now. Miss Charlotte will see you another time, when you—feel more composed.

(HE stumbles out the door.)

CHARLOTTE
    (To JAMES.)
I'm so sorry.

JAMES

No need to be sorry. It's obvious he's in love with you and brave to declare that love. Be kind to him. I must find Emily. There is something I must say to her before I go.

CHARLOTTE
Follow the path to Blackstone Crag. She'll be there.

JAMES
Thank you.
(HE exits.)

ANNE
Charlotte, are you all right?

CHARLOTTE
Mr. Nicholls has just proposed marriage.

ANNE
Oh, Charlotte. What will you tell him?

CHARLOTTE
I don't know.

END ACT I: SCENE THREE

ACT I: SCENE FOUR

(Late afternoon, the same day. The moors. EMILY is standing on Blackstone Edge.)

BRANWELL
(Entering.)
So you have returned to your kingdom. May I enter, oh Queen?

EMILY
The Prince of Angria has not visited Gondolan in a long time.

BRANWELL
No, not for a long time. It is as bleak and wild as ever. Thank God, there's something in this world that doesn't change.

EMILY
Something is troubling you. What is it?

BRANWELL
Everything! There are times when I have felt that other world spinning and toppling about my head, and I've only held onto sanity by clutching at this eye in the whirlwind—this center of loneliness and peace where nothing ever changes. Oh, Emily, If only we could go back to when we were children and begin again. When you were truly the Queen of Gondolan.

EMILY
And you were my prince. We built our castle here on these heights.

BRANWELL
And you planted flowers in the crevices of the rocks. I thought there was magic in your touch and you could make flowers grow from stones. There on that pinnacle, I used to stand look-out and challenge the terrible monsters hidden in the secret caves

EMILY
And the furious battles you waged on our behalf. You were wounded in a thousand places and how stoically you suffered your pain.

BRANWELL
I used to make Anne cry because she thought the monsters were real.

EMILY
And Charlotte would dry her tears and tell her the monsters were not real but only stories we made up.

BRANWELL
But now we know that they are all too real.

EMILY
Yes, now we know.

BRANWELL
Do you remember the snake we found—there on that ledge? When I wanted to crush it with a rock, you hit me with a stick and swore you'd kill me if I harmed it. I still have the scar where you drew blood!

EMILY
I meant to kill you. I coolly calculated just how I should do it.

BRANWELL
And just how did you intend to kill me?

EMILY
With your own sword.

BRANWELL
Perhaps you have.
   (Thoughtful pause.)

There are times when I've wished I could shed my skin and start over again.

EMILY

Can you?

BRANWELL

I don't know. Do you think I can?

EMILY

I'm not sure about you, Branwell, but I don't think I can.

(THEY are silent for a moment.)

BRANWELL

I've—I've written a few poems lately. I hadn't written anything in a long time. You know that's what terrified me.

EMILY

I know.

BRANWELL

All of us had that talent when we were children. And then, I lost it and I don't know where or why. It was the one thing that made life bearable, and I lost it.

EMILY

I know.

BRANWELL

But just lately, I've been writing again—just a poem here and there—but I think they're good. I really think they are good. Listen.

Nothing is as it seemed to be.
We plunge slowly earthward, arms for wings.
All that we can see are far stars spiraling.

We tread air and drown in leaves.
Yesterdays, like comets, flash.
Nothing is as it seemed to be,
Rose fire blooming into ash.

EMILY

Nothing is as it seemed to be.
We plunge slowly earthward, arms for wings....

BRANWELL

Do you—do you like it?

EMILY

I like it very much, Branwell.

BRANWELL

You aren't just saying that to heal the hurt feelings of a less talented brother?

EMILY

You know that I always try to be honest with you.

BRANWELL

Yes, I can always look to you for the truth. When I've lost my way and the fog closes around me, I know you will be my truth though I have none of my own.

EMILY

Oh, Branwell, I don't have your truth. I can't give you what I don't possess. You must find the truth in your own heart, or you'll not find it at all. Does the moor-lark ask for your truth, or does the rabbit shivering with fear in the bracken? They live and they die and that is their truth. You must find your own, or you won't find it at all.

BRANWELL
But can I—dare I—trust my heart?

EMILY
We dare not trust anything else!

BRANWELL
Oh, Emily, there are times when I could devour the world if I had the power! I could taste all the pleasures and find them sweet! But it's all turned to dust and ashes!
  (Pause.)
Do you really want the truth? I once loved you with all my heart. I would give my soul to have written *Wuthering Heights*, but you wrote it instead, and I've hated you for it. So, you see, you have killed me with my own sword. We should have stayed in our kingdom—loved and beloved—just as we were then!

EMILY
Oh, Prince of Angria, I, your Queen, command you. Take up your noble sword and follow me.
  (SHE begins to climb the rock face.)
There is no other path to freedom except over Blackstone Edge.
  (BRANWELL starts to follow HER. JAMES enters.)
Follow me! To the very top!

JAMES
Emily! Emily! Be careful!

  (EMILY climbs higher.)

BRANWELL
  (Climbs higher by a different path.)
Come on, Emily. Don't let him stop you!

EMILY

What's the matter, James Taylor? Can't you follow us? Are you afraid? Go back to your dark city. This is the only path to freedom over Blackstone Edge!

> (SHE leads BRANWELL higher onto the crags.)

BRANWELL

Come on, Emily!

> (THEY climb higher, JAMES watching from below, downstage.)

We'll climb the sky and shake the bars of heaven!

JAMES

Emily! Emily! Don't!

> (Taking a giant stride, BRANWELL misses HIS footing and falls to a stony ledge.)

EMILY

Branwell! Branwell!

> (EMILY rushes to HIS side as HE attempts to rise. HE is obviously not badly hurt, but has sprained HIS foot.)

BRANWELL

Leave me alone! I don't need your help! Take your hands off me or I'll kill you!

> (HE looks as though HE would willingly strike HER. THEY glare at EACH OTHER for a long moment. Then HE turns and hobbles painfully down the path, exiting.)

JAMES

(To EMILY.)

Are you all right?

EMILY

Oh, James, what am I? I wanted him to climb higher. I wanted him to reach the top, or I wanted him to fall—to die! To be gone from my life!

JAMES

Let me help you.

EMILY

Leave me alone! Every human I've ever known gives me what I don't want and asks what I can't give.

(JAMES moves toward HER.)

No! Do not mistake me. I mean what I am saying. I don't want you here. Leave me alone! Go back to your London! Get out of my life.

(After a long moment, JAMES turns away from her and exits.)

END ACT I: SCENE FOUR

END ACT I

ACT II: SCENE ONE

The Bronte sitting room. Early afternoon.

(EMILY is writing at the desk. SHE holds aloft the manuscript she has been working on.)

EMILY

There! It's finished! *Blackstone Edge*!
> (SOUND of the Moorlark SINGING in its cage. SHE crosses to the cage.)

Ah, my sweet, are you singing for joy? Are you happy?
> (SHE puts the manuscript on the desk and throws open the window. SUNLIGHT floods in.)

Look, the sun is shining and the heather is in bloom. One day the wild larks will call to you and you will no longer be able to deny the longing of your wild heart. Ah, my moorlark, tell me your secret—is it that you are truly happy in this moment no matter what chill winds are sure to follow spring?
> (SHE opens the cage.)

There! You can fly now if they call to you. You can fly now while you are singing for joy. No? You will not go? You will not leave me yet a while?
> (ANNE enters. SHE is wearing a cape and a bonnet.)

What a beautiful day! Anything could happen!

ANNE

What could happen?

EMILY

> (Takes ANNE'S hands and dances HER around and around.)

We will find the little people and make them let us dance in their ring. We will learn their secret of enchantment and how they capture mortals and never let them return.

ANNE

Oh, Emily, you take my breath away. How I love to hear you gay and laughing. When you're like this no one could deny you anything, not even the little people.

EMILY

Come with me, Anne.

ANNE

I can't. I promised Tabby I'd go to the village for her.
(CHARLOTTE enters.)
Won't you come, Charlotte? The walk will do you good.

CHARLOTTE

No, there isn't time. There is a great deal I have to do.

ANNE

Shall I bring you anything?

CHARLOTTE

Yes, a magic ring that makes wishes come true.

ANNE

I'll order one especially for you.

CHARLOTTE

No need to hurry. I'm sure they're out of stock.

ANNE

Then I'll bring you a surprise.

(SHE starts to exit.)

CHARLOTTE

Before you go, there's something of a surprise that I have to tell you both.

(SHE hesitates.)
Arthur Nicholls has asked me to marry him. I have decided to accept his proposal.

                    ANNE
Arthur Nicholls? Oh, Emily! Isn't that wonderful!

            (EMILY turns away and closes the door of the cage.)

                    CHARLOTTE
I thought you would be surprised.

                    ANNE
Oh, Charlotte, I saw the way he looked at you. Mr. Nicholls is very kind and very good.

                    CHARLOTTE
Yes, he is kind. And I shall try to be a good wife to him.

                    ANNE
I am so happy for both of you.

                    CHARLOTTE
Thank you, my dear. Now go on your errands.

            (ANNE exits.)

                    CHARLOTTE
                    (To EMILY.)
You're not congratulating me.

                    EMILY
You don't love Arthur Nicholls. Your heart still longs for Brussels and M. Heger.

CHARLOTTE
What good is longing for him! You know that he's married! I should never have loved him! I was a fool!

EMILY
Or not foolish enough. You should have told him.

CHARLOTTE
Told him? This past winter I wrote M. Heger letter after letter pouring out my heart to him. He never replied. My last letter was returned unopened. So you see, I was foolish enough. But I won't be a fool any longer. I realize that I've been living in a romantic dream of M. Heger who will never love me. And so, I have decided to marry Arthur Nicholls.

EMILY
You don't love Arthur Nicholls.

CHARLOTTE
Oh, Emily, I thought you, of all people, would understand. I'm afraid—afraid to be alone. Last night I had the same dream that I dream again and again.

EMILY
Your old nightmare?

CHARLOTTE
I am alone on the moor and I call and call your names. "Emily—Emily!" I call. "Branwell! Anne!" And the wind blows the words back into my face, and the cold and the darkness and the silence close about me. I am lost and alone and I want to weep, but no tears will come. I feel that you have all gone away, thoughtless and carefree, and left me desolate and alone. If I can only find you again, all will be well.

EMILY
(Embraces her.)
I am still here with you.

CHARLOTTE
I can't bear that anything should come between us. I think you are the closest thing to my heart in this world, Emily.

EMILY
And you are close to my heart. And nothing need come between us in this life unless we let it.

CHARLOTTE
Then why can't it be as it once was—when we read each other's work and shared our thoughts.

EMILY
I am not sure you would really want to share my true thoughts.

CHARLOTTE
Oh, but I would!

EMILY
The novel I have been writing all winter is finished. I have decided to let Mr. Taylor take the manuscript to London when he returns.

CHARLOTTE
Oh, Emily, perhaps this is the way out for all of us!

EMILY
I don't think you would want him to publish it as it is.

CHARLOTTE
Not publish it, but of course I....

EMILY
(SHE hands the manuscript to CHARLOTTE.)
Because it's about us.

CHARLOTTE
What do you mean it's about us?

EMILY
You and me and Father and Anne and the truth about Branwell. It is about our life here at Haworth and about you and M. Heger in Brussels. It is sometimes an ugly and a cruel story, and it is as true as I can bear.

CHARLOTTE
Oh, Emily, you can't mean to reveal our pain and anguish to the world for people to whisper about.

EMILY
That is just what I mean to do.

CHARLOTTE
Oh, no—not about my feelings for M. Heger!

EMILY
Yes, that, too. It is all there.

CHARLOTTE
Why must you do this? Why? Why?

EMILY
I must speak the truth in my heart, Charlotte, if I am to live!

CHARLOTTE
But what of Father? When he hears of what you have written for all to see, it would cut him to the heart.

EMILY
You know he never reads our novels. He assumes they are light and frivolous, hardly worth his time.

CHARLOTTE
But when he hears of what you have written, he would read it. Everyone would read it! Why must you do it?

EMILY
We are as we are, Charlotte. Whether I write about it or not, that won't change.

CHARLOTTE
(Throws the manuscript on the desk as if rejecting it.)
I am so tired of your selfishness and your stoicism that can so often only be justification for doing just as you please!

EMILY
Call it what you will.

CHARLOTTE
What will Mr. Taylor think of us when he reads this?

EMILY
Do you care what he thinks?

CHARLOTTE
Yes, I do! He comes from a different world. How could he understand what life has been like for us?

EMILY
Perhaps he could understand more than you think. But that, like everything else, is something we cannot change.

CHARLOTTE
You demand too much of us! You think we all have your courage. But we are not all as strong as you. You are too hard and unyielding. I can't bear anymore. I can't bear it!

EMILY
Oh, but you can, my dearest. You will stand fast and bear it 'til we are all in the earth.

CHARLOTTE
Hush, don't say that! I won't hear it.

EMILY
All right, then, I won't say it. And I won't be made unhappy and drowned in tears today. Like my moorlark, today I will be happy. Feel the sunshine, smell the heather! I think it is a magic day. The earth is holding her breath—waiting for....

CHARLOTTE
Waiting for what?

EMILY
Waiting for her lover to fill her to overflowing and bear the spring in her arms.

CHARLOTTE
Emily!

EMILY
Are you shocked? I like to shock you just to erase the frown from your face. Come with me, Charlotte, to Blackstone Edge as we used to. When each day lasted forever!

CHARLOTTE
Your swift change of mood is too much for me. It really isn't fair of you.

EMILY

But nothing is fair! Fair is a will-o'-the-wisp that leads you in circles only to vanish when you are lost. Oh, Charlotte, take the frown off your face. Be happy now.

CHARLOTTE

No, You're being—childish!

EMILY

Childish—childlike—so I am! This day will never come again. Don't you understand? This is my brief and only spring, and I'll not deny it.

(SHE exits.)

CHARLOTTE

Emily! Emily!

(CHARLOTTE turns away angrily. She looks at the manuscript on the desk. SHE crosses and picks it up, and looks intently at the cover. SHE begins to open it, and then throws it on the desk and turns away angrily.

TABBY

(Entering.)

Miss Charlotte.

CHARLOTTE

Oh, you startled me! My nerves seem to be bad today.

TABBY

Branwell's in the kitchen with the smell of drink on his breath. I don't know what will happen if he's like this when your father comes home.

CHARLOTTE
I thought Branwell went to the village this morning.

TABBY
He did. But now he's back and the worse for it.

CHARLOTTE
How bad is he?

TABBY
He's not crazy like he gets sometimes. Just enough to loosen his tongue.

BRANWELL
(Appearing in the doorway.)
Your servant, ladies!
(Makes a mock bow.)

CHARLOTTE
(SHE places the manuscript on the desk.)
Branwell, you know what Father told you last time if you appeared in the house drunk.

BRANWELL
I could recite by heart his usual sermon. I saw him approaching the Black Bull, and to avoid our esteemed Father, I ducked out the back way with a word to the landlord to be none the wiser.

CHARLOTTE
What is he going to say now when he sees you at home during working hours?

BRANWELL
What has he always said? And what difference has it made? I may decide to go up to London after all.

TABBY

London, is it? If wishes were horses, we all would ride to London!

BRANWELL

When I go up to London
I'm going to do the town!
London Bridge won't be a-falling.
It's the ladies'll come tumbling down!

CHARLOTTE

Branwell!

TABBY
(To BRANWELL.)

Wishin's easy, but the doin's hard, I'm thinkin'.

(SHE exits.)

BRANWELL
(With a broad leer.)

That doing had better be!

CHARLOTTE

Branwell! This is not a burlesque stage!

BRANWELL

Of course, that's it! I've found my career! My sister novelists will create, while I burlesque their worthy creations on the stages of the unworthy world! Is your Mr. Taylor coming? I'll have him recommend me to a London producer!

CHARLOTTE

He would not recommend you for anything after the scene you made when he first arrived.

BRANWELL
To hell with your Mr. Taylor. If I do decide to go to London, I won't need his help. I'm fed up with this god-forsaken place! The high point in the day is when the church bell rings noon and everyone cheeks his clock. "Well, what do you know, two minutes fast, Mrs. Creevy!"
(Noticing the manuscript on the desk.)
Well, what is this, Charlotte? Have you manufactured another satanic Mr. Rochester and long-suffering Jane Eyre?

CHARLOTTE
It's -- Emily's new novel. She's going to send it to London with Mr. Taylor.

BRANWELL
(Picking up the manuscript.)
Emily's new novel, is it? God, to have one sister who writes is bad enough, but three! They turn out novels like bread loaves between breakfast and tea!

(HE starts to turn the pages.)

CHARLOTTE
(Alarmed.)
Emily doesn't want us to read it. She said so particularly.

BRANWELL
And of course you wouldn't violate her trust. God, you're impossible, Charlotte!

CHARLOTTE
You mustn't read it, Branwell.

BRANWELL
Now you've aroused my curiosity. Why the urgent tone, Charlotte? Are you afraid I'll be even more envious than I am already?

CHARLOTTE
Branwell, please don't read it.

BRANWELL
Blackstone Edge—our Blackstone Edge? Well!
(He turns to the first page and reads.)
"The four of them had grown up on the edge of the Yorkshire Moor, knowing no society but their own, and the wild moor that began just beyond their door. Cordelia, Brumley, Eve, and Amy—from their earliest childhood it was as if they were fated to their existence by dark gods more ancient and inexorable than the moor itself. I speak of all four children, but I will speak mainly of one—Brumley, the only son."
(HE reads on silently and gradually becomes more and more agitated.)
Do you know what she's written here? God damn her soul to hell! Does she think she can play God? What right does she have to be me? Do you know what she's written here?

CHARLOTTE
I haven't read it. But I know that it's about—us.

BRANWELLL
I'm surrounded by people who think they can tell me how to live my life! Am I your surrogate to the world for the sins you're all afraid to commit? With your insufferable female simpering it's always, "Poor Branwell this, and poor Branwell that." Whatever I do you complain of and then scribble it quickly in your notebooks without ever having the guts to live it yourselves! Does she think she can embalm me in the pages of her book along with her unsatisfied desires? If anyone writes my story it will be me, just as I've been the one to live it! She's already stolen my soul! She won't steal my life from me, too!

TABBY
(Entering, agitated.)
Your father has just ridden into the stable yard, and there's a storm cloud in his face.

CHARLOTTE
Branwell, don't let him see you like this.

BRANWELL
God damn you all and him most of all! I've been his surrogate, too, for all his unsatisfied dreams and desires, and I'll have no more of it! If he looks for genius and talent, let him search his own soul. I won't play the part anymore! Get yourselves another black sheep!

(HE throws the manuscript onto the desk.)

TABBY
You'd best be gone while you can, or you'll bring a storm on all our heads.

BRANWELL
Stay out of this, Tabby. I don't need any more interference in my life!

MR. BRONTE
(Entering.)
Tabby, you may go back to the kitchen.

TABBY
Yes, sir.

(SHE exits.)

MR. BRONTE
Charlotte, would you leave us alone, please!

CHARLOTTE
Oh, Father, please wait until we are all calmer. We are all to upset now.

BRANWELL

You stay out of this, Charlotte. I'm sick of your eternally picking up the pieces and your insufferable martyrdom for all the world like one of your long-suffering heroines.

MR. BRONTE

That is enough! I hear in the village that you've been discharged from Manchester and Leeds for repeated dereliction of duty.

BRANWELL

Dereliction of duty is it? That wasn't what you expected of me, was it, Father? Not of your boy genius. I should have been an artist or a famous poet at the very least!

MR. BRONTE

That is enough, I said!

BRANWELL

No, it isn't nearly enough. For the funny part is that it's true! I should have been an artist or a poet at the very least and therefore I refuse to make my life a row of numbers in a ledger to gather dust at Manchester and Leeds. If that truth disappoints you, then let it. At least I'm consistent. When have I ever been anything but a disappointment to you? But I don't care anymore.

MR. BRONTE

That does not surprise me. It has been a long time since you've cared about anyone but yourself. You make a very fine speech about being too proud to do an honest day's work as a clerk, but you are not too proud to take money from this house and spend the day drinking at the Black Bull. What will happen to your sisters when I am gone with no man in the house?

BRANWELL

My sisters? Even if they took to walking the streets of London, they'd probably scribble it all in their notebooks and make a fortune writing it into a novel. And it might be the making of them as women.

> MR. BRONTE
> (Enraged, clutching Branwell's shirt, ready to strike HIM.)

God help you! God help you!

> (THEY struggle TOGETHER.)

> BRANWELL

Get your hands off me or I'll kill you! I'll kill you!

> CHARLOTTE

Oh! Don't! Don't!

> MR. BRONTE
> (Throwing BRANWELL against the door.)

Get out of this house! I don't ever want to see you again in this life or, God help you, in the next.

> BRANWELL

God help you, Father. He gave up on me a long time ago. Don't worry—you won't see me again, in this life or the next. Not if I can help it! If you are destined for heaven, I much prefer Hell.

> (BRANWELL starts for the door, but then notices EMILY'S manuscript on the table. HE looks at it for a moment, then defiantly walks over and picks it up. CHARLOTTE tries to stop HIM, but his fierce glance warns her away. BRANWELL exits.)

END ACT II: SCENE ONE

ACT II: SCENE TWO

(Mid-afternoon. The moor.)

EMILY
(Sitting alone in HER favorite spot.)

There is no time for tears,
While springtime stars are burning
While evening sheds its silent dew
Or sunshine gilds the morning.

Spring retreats and from its fate
My fate cannot be severed.
But this one day of springtime
Will stay in my heart forever.
This one day of springtime
Will stay in my heart forever.

JAMES
(Entering.)
Emily. Emily. I knew you'd be here, and I came to find you.

EMILY
Yes, I knew you'd come.

JAMES
How did you know?

EMILY
Because today is a magic day when anything could happen! Can't you feel its magic?

JAMES
Perhaps Tabby's little people are near.

EMILY

I saw them once—long ago when I was a child. A long time ago. I know the secret of their enchantment.

JAMES

If you know their secret, you must tell me.

EMILY

It is only to be alive in this moment that is all we have. Oh, don't you feel alive, alive today? Look! There is lightning in the air! It tingles along my nerves and I am trembling in its power! Look there—the storm clouds gathering over the far crags. They'll be here before morning.
    (Stands, listening.)
Listen, the moorlark is calling to her mate and the earth is holding her breath, waiting—waiting.

JAMES

Waiting for what?

EMILY

For the storm to fill her to overflowing and bear the spring in her arms.

> (JAMES draws HER to him and is just about to kiss her. BRANWELL enters suddenly from behind a ledge.)

BRANWELL

How charming! Awakening love! How very charming indeed. And will you go off to London then, Emily, with your lover and live happily ever after? Do you always win? Life and love and fame? Why does fortune smile only on you? Who chose you to be the winner? Who elected you?

EMILY

What is it, Branwell? What has happened?

BRANWELL

Happened? How do you know anything has happened? How do you presume to know?

EMILY

Because you are here, and I see it in your face, and I hear it in your voice.

BRANWELL

Why no, you're wrong, my dear sister. Nothing has happened of any importance to anyone. Oh, my father has thrown me out of the house and damned me to Hell, and you have stolen my soul. But it is nothing of importance at all. It is only that my disembodied ghost refuses to bury the corpse. My corpse insists upon walking about—see, here it is.

EMILY

You've read my manuscript! You should not have read it, Branwell.

BRANWELL

God damn you! God damn you to hell! What right have you to make me into one of your characters.

JAMES

Shut your filthy mouth!

BRANWELL

Stay out of this.

EMILY

Please, James, this is between Branwell and myself.

BRANWELL
What right have you to steal my life?

EMILY
You said once yourself—it is the truth that hurts the most. I had no choice, Branwell. I had to write the truth as I see it.

BRANWELL
Who gave you the truth? What special holy revelation have you had? Be careful what you do, Emily. You have no right to pretend to my story. You have no right to bare my soul. Do your own undressing!

EMILY
It is my story, too, Branwell. If you see yourself mirrored there then I have caught something of the truth and I cannot change that truth, anymore than I can change the fate you and I share.

BRANWELL
I won't be caught in your fate or in your spell! I want to be alive, and breathe and feel, not already dead, a character in some other time and place!

EMILY
But we are both—don't you see? Alive now and already dead in some other time and place. And we can't change it. It's been lived already, and long before, and will be lived again and again.

BRANWELL
No! No! I won't believe that! Damn your truth and your fate that sees into my soul!
    (As if to threaten HER, HE grabs HER arms. JAMES steps between THEM. BRANWELL and JAMES struggle. JAMES throws BRANWELL to the ground.)

JAMES

Get out of here! If you ever threaten her again and I hear of it, you'll answer to me.

BRANWELL
(Sitting up, regarding JAMES with contempt.)

I could bloody this moor with you! I have a strength you know nothing of!

(HE springs to HIS feet.)

But I have other business today, other prospects you know nothing about!

(HE turns to leave, then stops momentarily and turns back to EMILY.)

I'm not dead yet, Emily. Remember that! I'm not dead yet!

(HE exits.)

JAMES
(Crossing to EMILY.)

Did he hurt you, my darling?

EMILY

It doesn't matter. I'm all right. Oh, James, he's so afraid! He knows and he's afraid! And so am I! So am I! I'm not as brave as I seem.

JAMES

Oh, my darling! You're trembling.

EMILY

Oh, James, hold me! Hold me! Don't let me go!

(HE takes HER in HIS arms. THEY cling there together.)

END ACT II: SCENE TWO

ACT II: SCENE THREE

(Late afternoon. The back room of the Black Bull. The LANDLORD is in the archway. HE calls to NAT who is OFF, preparing to leave.)

LANDLORD
Nat, has it started to rain?

NAT
(Voice OFF.)
Not yet. But there are thunder heads over Old Blacky, and we'll be havin' a real blow before morning, I'm thinkin'. My hip is aching somethin' fierce.

LANDLORD
Your old woman will want you to warm her bed with the storm comin' on. Women do get skittish with lightning in the air.

NAT
(Voice OFF.)
I better be gettin' home afore the storm breaks.

LANDLORD
Branwell, mi lad!

BRANWELL
(Entering.)
Ah, mine host of the Black Bull! Drinks all around and a special pint for my good friend, Nat.

NAT
(Voice OFF.)
I was just leavin', lad.

BRANWELL

You'll stay and have a drink with me surely!

NAT

(Voice OFF.)

Can't, lad. My old woman will be expectin' me long since.

BRANWELL

Keep 'em guessing and you keep the upper hand, Nat.

NAT

(Voice OFF.)

Eh, that's a true word, but she does aim a wicked broomstick

LANDLORD

I'll wish you a quick journey then before the storm catches you on the roads.

BRANWELL

(To LANDLORD.)

Ah, my friend, serve us a pint in here before the fire. There's a chill in the air you can feel in your bones.

LANDLORD

Aye, that's a fact.

BRANWELL

This is a farewell drink we'll be having. You'll drink to my health and good fortune.

LANDLORD

A farewell drink, you're saying, Branwell? Are you leavin' us then?

BRANWELL

Here's to the bawdy, bustling, brave city of London and to all her enchantments.

(HE lifts HIS drink.)
To London.

LANDLORD
London, is it?

BRANWELL
I'm off to make my fortune. When next you see me, I'll be wearing a tall silk hat and be sitting in a coach and pair, driving through Hyde Park.

LANDLORD
With a lass on each arm, I'll be bound. Will your silver tongue pay your lodgings in London?

BRANWELL
You've hit it exactly. That's the currency in London. My silver tongue and this!
    (HE throws Emily's manuscript onto the table.)
That's my ticket to fame and fortune! The cost runs high, but it will buy me my freedom from Haworth moor.

LANDLORD
What is it, mi lad? Some kind o' book?
    (HE picks up the manuscript.)
Do they pay you for writin' books?

BRANWELL
Pay you—why, man you can get rich overnight! With this book, I'll be the new Lord Byron!

LANDLORD
Lord Byron is it?

BRANWELL
He was the most famous author in all of England. He led the life

he wanted to lead and didn't give a damn what any of them said. He set all the tongues to wagging and the women fell at his feet. He could have his pick.

LANDLORD

Was, you say? Then what good's his writin' to him if he's dead? Or to his women? They won't grieve long in a cold bed. The only way you can keep 'em is if you're alive and frisky.

BRANWELL

I always knew you were a philosopher, my friend. I'll drink to your philosophy. It's the wisest I've heard this day.

LANDLORD

So it's a book you've written, is it? You'll be famous one day, mark my words.
      (Reading the title.)
Blackstone Edge. Is that the title of your book, Branwell?

BRANWELL

It's the book I've always wanted to write. It's a great book—a work of genius that lays bare the heart of man and looks into his soul. I'll drink a toast to this book. Its author will be remembered as long as men can read and hearts can feel. Its author will live on in spirit when you and I are dead and gone from this earth!

LANDLORD

Hear! Hear! To your book! And to your prosperity! I'll say one day I drank a pint to your health around this very table. With the very book lyin' there between us that changed his life and proved his worth. If anyone can do it, you can, me lad.

BRANWELL

      (Going to the fireplace.)
Yes, the very book that changed his life and proved his worth.
      (HIS manner has changed.)

LANDLORD

It won't be the same without you, Branwell, and that's the truth. The tradesmen coming through have heard tell you spin the best yarns this side o' Leeds.

BRANWELL

I'll be expecting someone here tonight. You understand, Landlord?

LANDLORD

Your lady friend, is it? Shall I be fixin' the upstairs room for you then?

BRANWELL

Indeed. But join me in another pint first.
> (LANDLORD exits. There is the SOUND OFF of someone entering the bar room. BRANWELL crosses to the window and looks out. LANDLORD enters, reluctantly.)

Is she here? Where is she?

LANDLORD

Her coachman was just here. He's come and gone. He said to give you a message
> (HE hesitates.)

BRANWELL

> (Again rushing to the window to look out.)

What did he say? Can't she come?

LANDLORD

He said to give you this message.

BRANWELL

What message? Tell me! Tell me!

LANDLORD
I'm to tell you that if you come on her lands again, she'll give orders to the servants that the dogs are to be set on you and you're to be shot as an intruder.

BRANWELL
(Grabbing the LANDLORD by the shirt.)
That's a lie! It's her husband sent that message.

LANDLORD
She said to give you this miniature you painted of her. That way you'd know the message was from her.
(HE hands BRANWELL the miniature.)

BRANWELL
(HE stares at the miniature as if HE cannot comprehend then throws the miniature against the wall.)
That lying bitch! Afraid to lose his lands and fortune! She'll ache for me in her cold bed on the long nights to come with only her lands to warm her. There will come a day when she'll look in the mirror and give all she owns to be in my arms again. She can go to hell for all I care!

LANDLORD
Branwell, lad....

BRANWELL
None of that! I don't need your pity. Bring me a bottle of Jamaica rum.
(LANDLORD exits. BRANWELL stands bowed over the table. Then HE picks up the manuscript and looks at it.)
And you, Emily, I damn you to Hell as well! See what it is to burn!

(BRANWELL deliberately walks to the fireplace and hurls the manuscript into the flames. LAND-

LORD enters with the bottle of rum. HE puts it on the table, then notices the manuscript in the fire.)

LANDLORD
Branwell, lad, you're burning your book!

(HE stoops down to retrieve the manuscript, but BRANWELL stops him.)

BRANWELL
Leave it! I want to know how the Devil feels when he burns souls! Get out! Get out!

(LANDLORD rises slowly, looks for a moment at BRANWELL, and then exits. BRANWELL stands looking into the fire for a moment, then crosses to the table, picks up the bottle and takes a long drink. LIGHTS DIM then SLOWLY RISE. Some time has passed. BRANWELL is seated at the table, HIS head in HIS arms. The rum bottle is lying on its side on the table. There is a BRIGHT FLASH OF LIGHTNING followed by a LOUD CLAP OF THUNDER.)

BRANWELL
(Aroused by the noise.)
What—what's that?

(HE raises HIS head slowly, looks all about, and then staggers drunkenly to HIS feet, knocking the bottle to the floor.)

LANDLORD
(Having heard the bottle drop and coming to the archway to check on BRANWELL.)
What is it? Are you all right, lad?

BRANWELL
(Barely able to focus on LANDLORD.)
What's that? What did you say?

LANDLORD
Are you all right, lad? Are you all right?

BRANWELL
Why wouldn't I be all right? Bring me another bottle of rum.

LANDLORD
You'd better take a rest, lad.

BRANWELL
Don't want a rest. Didn't you hear me? Bring me another bottle!

LANDLORD
(Going to BRANWELL and attempting to lead HIM back to the chair at the table.)
Come on, lad. Just a little nap. Do you good.

BRANWELL
(Breaking loose.)
No! No time for a nap! Have other business today.
(HE looks about, first puzzled, and then wildly searching.)
Where's her book? What have you done with her book?
(HE grabs LANDLORD fiercely by the collar.)

LANDLORD
You burned it, lad! You burned it! There in the fireplace. It's ashes now!

BRANWELL
Emily's book? I burned it? Ashes now?
(Stares into the fireplace.)
It's all ashes now!

LANDLORD
(After a long moment.)
I tried to stop you, lad. But you wouldn't let me.

BRANWELL
(Still staring into the fireplace.)
I—I....
(Suddenly resolute.)
I've got to go. Got to go—home.

LANDLORD
(Taking BRANWELL'S arm.)
No, lad. You'd better stop the night here. It's storming outside somethin' fierce. You're in no condition to go out. Stop the night here!

BRANWELL
(Shaking loose from LANDLORD.)
Leave me alone! Get out of my way!
(HE stumbles against the chair and knocks it over on HIS way to the door.)
I've got to go. Got to go home.

(When BRANWELL opens the door, a strong wind pushes the door further open. BRANWELL exits, leaving the door open. A FLASH OF LIGHTNING ILLUMINATES the room.)

LANDLORD
(Rushing to the door and trying to call after HIM over the noise of the storm.)
Branwell, lad! Come back! Come back!

(Finally, with difficulty, the LANDLORD closes the door against the wind.)

END ACT II: SCENE THREE

ACT II: SCENE FOUR

(Some days later, afternoon, the Bronte sitting room. CHARLOTTE enters and stands looking out the window.)

ANNE
(Entering.)
Charlotte, I can't get Father to rest.

CHARLOTTE
I know. Night after night by Branwell's side. I asked Tabby to go up for a while.

ANNE
How are you feeling, my dear?

CHARLOTTE
Oh, Anne, I don't know what has been the matter with me these last days. I simply can't take hold as I used to.

ANNE
You are feeling better, though.

CHARLOTTE
I've been lying in bed these days past, watching the rain fall, remembering how it was when we were children. The long rainy afternoons before the fire when we wrote together and created our own kingdom. Do you remember how good those days were.

ANNE
Yes, I remember.

CHARLOTTE
You were always the young princess who had to be rescued, and now you have been taking care of all of us.

ANNE

But you're much better and will be your old self again.

CHARLOTTE

Yes, I'm much better, but what of Emily? Oh, Anne, she has been so very ill. The night she brought Branwell home, raging with fever and delirium, they were both soaked through with the cold and the storm. It frightens me to look into her eyes.

ANNE

We should ask Dr. Evans to see her when he comes.

CHARLOTTE

It won't do any good. She would only refuse to see him.

ANNE

Mr. Taylor has come everyday, asking about Branwell. He said that he would go back to London until she sees him.

CHARLOTTE

What did she say?

ANNE

She made me promise not to tell him that she has been ill.

CHARLOTTE

Oh, Anne....

ANNE

Hush, now. It will be all right.

CHARLOTTE

Will it? I used to think we could escape—go away to London or Brussels—and make another life somehow. But I know now we'll never escape.

EMILY
(Entering.)
I heard voices downstairs and thought Mr. Taylor was here.

CHARLOTTE
Emily, you shouldn't be up. You've been ill and feverish.

EMILY
Fever makes one light-headed, Charlotte, and our oh-so-stable world begins to dissolve like mist in morning sunshine. Did you know that?

CHARLOTTE
You must let me send for Dr. Evans.

EMILY
I'll send for him when it is time.

ANNE
I'll fix tea. Would you like that?

EMILY
Yes, thank you. I'll just rest here a while.

> (CHARLOTTE and ANNE exit. EMILY collapses on the sofa, HER back against the cushion. After a moment MR. BRONTE enters.)

MR. BRONTE
Are you feeling better, my dear?

EMILY
Yes, Father.

MR. BRONTE
Forgive me. These past days, I have thought only of Branwell.

(HE bows his head.)
How can I lead my congregation to find faith when I cannot see my own way in the dark.

EMILY
I believe your faith will walk with you through the valley of the shadow.

MR. BRONTE
I pray God that it does. Branwell has changed so. At the eleventh hour, he has found a new strength. He has given a lesson to us all.

EMILY
Yes, he has given a lesson to us all.

MR. BRONTE
You and your sisters have been much in my thoughts. I'm afraid that I have taught you to distrust the world outside these lonely walls.

EMILY
Yes, you have taught your lesson well.

MR. BRONTE
But I, too, can learn. One day when I am gone, you will need a man in the house. I shall send for Arthur Nicholls at High Cross. I'll no longer stand in their way if Charlotte will have him.

EMILY
Don't wait too long, Father.

MR. BRONTE
Yes, you are right. I'll send for him today. When Branwell is well again and Charlotte is settled, you and Anne and I—we'll travel about and see something of England and Ireland. Would you like that?

EMILY
Yes, Father, I would like that.

MR. BRONTE
I've wanted to go home to Ireland and see the house where I was born and the graves of my mother and father. I haven't been there since I was a boy.

EMILY
Yes, I think it is time to go.

MR. BRONTE
I'll tell your sisters of my decision. You must rest and regain your strength. I have many plans for all of us.

TABBY
(Entering.)
Branwell is calling for you, sir.

MR. BRONTE
I'm coming.

EMILY
Father. God be with you.

MR. BRONTE
God be with you, my brave heart.
(HE exits.)

TABBY
Mr. Taylor is in the kitchen. He has come at this same time every day. Will you see him this time?

EMILY
Yes, I'll see him.

(TABBY exits. EMILY puts the whole distance of the room between HERSELF and the door.)

JAMES
(Enters. For a long moment they do not speak.)
How is your brother?

EMILY
He will be well soon.

JAMES
That is very good news.

EMILY
Forgive me for not seeing you before, but I have not been receiving visitors.

JAMES
Am I only a "visitor"? I'll keep the length of the room between us if that's what you want, but you know, as I know, that space can't separate us.

EMILY
Only the mist on the moor, and the keen of the wind, and the cry of the lark in the grey sky.

JAMES
I won't believe that. When your brother is all well again, I want you to go with me to London

EMILY
Go with you to London?

JAMES
Yes, as my wife.

EMILY

Do you remember when we first met in this room?

JAMES

I'll never forget that moment.

EMILY

I said that you had a powerful rival. You thought he was a figure in my imagination, but he is real. I've known him all my life and I know now that I belong to him. I find in him a cruelty that matches and fulfills my cruel heart.

JAMES

I don't believe that. When we were together on the moors, you belonged to me then. I know that if I've ever known anything.

EMILY

For that moment only. I belong to him now. I've roamed the moors with him since I was a child. Once long ago, Branwell and I went up onto Blackstone Edge. The mist had risen from the valleys and as far as the eye could see the hills lay floating in the mist like islands in a purple sea. He and I vowed that one day we would sail that magic sea together. I see him there now on the high moor with the wind at his back. He is falling in the rain and turning with the stars and the sweet heather is growing from his wild heart.
    (A long pause.)
There is something I want to give you.
    (SHE crosses to the desk and takes out JAMES'
    letters.)
Here are your letters. Take them. They belong to you.

JAMES

You'll have to give them to me.
    (EMILY hesitates and then slowly crosses the room
    and holds out the letters. Suddenly HE steps forward and takes HER in HIS arms.)

Do you think your gypsy heart can deny life? I feel it beating here against me and your face is flushed as it was that day on the moor. Wherever you are, there is life.

EMILY
(Letting the letters drop to the floor.)
Oh, James, the room is toppling about me! I can't hold out anymore.

JAMES
Do you think I'll ever let you go?

EMILY
I'll always be with you. But promise me one thing. That you'll leave this house now and take the road to Keighley and go back to London. Send for me in two weeks time.

JAMES
And you'll promise to come to me?

EMILY
Yes. I'll be with you—always. Go now.

JAMES
I'll come back for you. And we'll go to London together.

EMILY
Yes. Go now.

(HE exits. EMILY stands for a moment. Then SHE picks up the letters, takes them to the fire and sets them ablaze.)

CHARLOTTE
(Enters.)
Emily, you sent him away.

EMILY
He's on his way back to London.

CHARLOTTE
Oh, Emily, don't send him away. Let me go after him. He loves you. Don't let him go.
    (SHE goes to the window.)
He's almost out of sight. Let me go after him. There's still time.

EMILY
No, let him go. Is he past the crossroads?

CHARLOTTE
Yes. I can't see him anymore.
    (Long pause.)
Will you rest now?

EMILY
Yes. I think you might send for the doctor now.

CHARLOTTE
Emily....

(THEY look at each other for a long moment.)

EMILY
It's all right, my dear. It has come right in the end.

TABBY
(Entering hurriedly.)
It's Branwell. He's calling for you. Come quickly.

(TABBY and CHARLOTTE exit.)

EMILY
(Crosses to the window and opens it. SHE opens

the door of the moorlark's cage.)
Will you go now while you are young and your heart calls to the open sky? There is nothing to hold you now. It is time to try your wings. The wild larks are calling and you are free.

(SHE releases the bird at the open window.)

ANNE
(At the door.)
Emily, you must hurry.

(THEY exit.)

END ACT II: SCENE FOUR

ACT II: SCENE FIVE

(BRANWELL'S bedroom. The set can be suggested, rather than a fully realized set. BRANWELL is lying on the bed. MR. BRONTE is sitting in a chair by the bed. CHARLOTTE enters and crosses to Branwell.)

BRANWELL
Charlotte—Charlotte?

CHARLOTTE
Yes, I'm here beside you. Rest—sh-h-h-h, rest.

(SHE puts HER hand on HIS forehead. HE seems to rest, and SHE turns from the bed. SHE moves some bottles on the bedside table, and the noise arouses MR. BRONTE. HE awakes with a start.)

MR. BRONTE
Is there any change?

CHARLOTTE
Only that he is strangely quiet. He called my name as I bathed his forehead. I think he knew me, but then he was quiet.

MR. BRONTE
Strangely quiet—yes, strangely quiet. It is only the end I have been expecting these months past. The nights I sat up with him in his drunken stupor—nights when he kept a gun by his bed threatening to kill us all and the mornings of remorse when it was all to be different.
 (Pause.)
And now—it is strangely different. The Branwell we knew is gone. Now he is like a child, helpless and without pretense. And now I am more terrified than I ever was in all the long nights of hell when we wrestled for his soul!

CHARLOTTE
He is resting now. Father, let us pray together.

MR. BRONTE
What shall I pray? Shall I pray "Thy will be done." Whether I will it or no? Shall I pray for Branwell's soul when I know that Branwell does not want me to meddle with his soul?
(Pause.)
Do you know, Charlotte, that I have loved this willful antagonist of my Lord—with all my heart?

CHARLOTTE
I know.

MR. BRONTE
As a boy, he was like I once was. I meant him to fulfill his many talents. If he had been weak-minded and poor-spirited, I could have understood—but with his talent—and to let it go to waste and lie fallow. And now to see him like this—to see him in his suffering become the boy he once was....

CHARLOTTE
You must get some rest, Father. You've been up for three days and nights without sleep. He's quiet now. At least try to sleep until the doctor comes.

MR. BRONTE
Rest—sleep? I have preached of Hell so often and now—for the first time my Lord has made me understand that Hell is in the human soul, and there—there is no escaping.
(BRANWELL stirs restlessly and moans. MR. BRONTE feels his forehead.)
Charlotte, see if Jacob has returned with the doctor.
(CHARLOTTE anxiously looks at BRANWELL and then exits. MR. BRONTE kneels by the bed.)
Branwell—oh, Branwell.

BRANWELL

Father—Father....

MR. BRONTE

Yes, yes—I am here—beside you. No, do not try to sit up. You have been very ill.

BRANWELL

I am better now. Can you forgive me now for the pain I've caused?

MR. BRONTE

Oh, my son, don't torture me.

BRANWELL

Say that you forgive me and let me go.

MR. BRONTE

I forgive you, but who—who will forgive me?

(CHARLOTTE and ANNE enter with TABBY.)

TABBY

Oh, Branwell, my cherub.

(SHE puts HER handkerchief to HER eyes and kneels on the other side of the bed. ANNE and CHARLOTTE cross to the bed. EMILY enters and stands back by the door, in the shadows.)

BRANWELL

Anne—my sweet Anne.

ANNE

Oh, Branwell—I love you.

BRANWELL
And I love you, my dear, and have loved you always. I couldn't tell you until now. Let me kiss you goodbye.

(ANNE kisses HIM and then collapses, kneeling by HIS bed, in TABBY'S arms.)

BRANWELL
Charlotte....

CHARLOTTE
(Taking HIS hand.)
Oh, Branwell....

BRANWELL
One more sorrow for you to take care of, Charlotte. But only one more from me. Perhaps it has come right in the end after all.

CHARLOTTE
Oh, Branwell, I cannot bear it.

BRANWELL
Yes, you can—and more. Sh-h-h now. How foolish it all was. Now I'd be willing to live. For I think if I should live now it would be different, but I won't live to find out. And that's all right, too.

CHARLOTTE
Oh, Branwell –
(SHE bows HER head, kneeling at the foot of HIS bed.)

BRANWELL
Are you there, Emily?
(HE tries to raise HIS head from the pillow, but SHE does not answer.)
Is that you there in the shadows?

(HE tries to focus on HER.)
Do you know what I did, Emily?

EMILY

Yes, I know.

BRANWELL

Do you know that I destroyed your manuscript?

EMILY

Yes, I know.

BRANWELL

It was all—true. And—I saw myself there—but I couldn't have written it. Do you hate me now, Emily?

EMILY

No, I don't hate you.

BRANWELL

You aren't kneeling with the others.
    (HE tries again to see HER more clearly.)
Nothing will make you kneel, will it, Emily? Not even—not even death. Is that your secret? Is that the answer?
    (HE pushes back the covers.)
Then I won't kneel, either. I have been on my knees long enough. For once I shall stand as a man.

    (Struggling, HE stands.)

CHARLOTTE

Branwell!
    (CHARLOTTE and MR. BRONTE try to support HIM.)

BRANWELL

No, don't help me! Let me stand!

(CHARLOTTE and MR. BRONTE step back and let HIM stand alone.)

I will stand on my feet as a man.

(Standing, weak but triumphant, HE looks around the room, then manages to focus on EMILY.)

Emily—there is one more monster to fight, and he is there in the shadows beside you! His wings touch your face! He is real! He raises his sword—and his face is fearful—and his dark wings spread out and out and cover the room. But his eyes, Emily, his eyes blaze like—like the morning sun!

(BRANWELL begins to fall, and EMILY rushes to HIS side and supports HIM as HE sinks to the floor.)

You are fighting by my side, aren't you, Emily?

EMILY

Yes, Branwell.

BRANWELL

Did we win, Emily?

EMILY

No...we lost.

(BRANWELL slumps to the floor and dies.) (Staring at BRANWELL, transfixed.)

But your eyes, too, blazed like the morning sun! And you are free.

END ACT II: SCENE FIVE

END ACT II

THE END

Appendix

The Moorlark
Workshops, Readings, and Awards and Honors

<u>Workshops and Readings</u>
2006 Utah Shakespeare Festival New American Playwrights Program, Cedar City, Utah. One week developmental workshop with Equity actors and director followed by three staged readings.
2004 Playwrights Collective New Play Series, Brookfield Theatre for the Arts, Connecticut.

<u>Awards and Honors</u>
2007 Nominated for the Susan Smith Blackburn National Prize.
2007 Semi-finalist, Orlando Shakespeare Harriett Lake Festival, Florida.
2006 Chosen for Utah Shakespeare Festival Plays in Progress.
2006 Chosen for Playwrights Collective New Play Series, Brookfield Theatre for the Arts, Connecticut.
2005 Honorable Mention (out of 18,000 entries), 74th Annual Writer's Digest Competition, Stage Play Category.
2004 Finalist, Northern Kentucky University.

About the Authors

Jan Henson Dow has won more than 150 national playwriting competitions, awards, and honors, including an NBC New Voices Award. Her plays have received numerous productions, workshops, and staged readings around the country, and her full-length plays have been published by Samuel French and Popular Play Service.

As a Professor at Western Connecticut State University, Dow directed the Playwriting Workshops and co-produced Western's Festival of New Plays. She has been the recipient of a number of playwriting grants, as well as grants for the new play festivals. She also taught playwriting workshops at the Osher Life Long Learning Institute at the University of South Carolina and at workshops around the country.

Her articles and poems have appeared in such publications as *The New York Times*, *The Dramatists Guild Quarterly*, *Kansas Quarterly*, and *Indiana Review*. She co-authored *Writing the Award Winning Play* with Shannon Michal Dow, and they have just completed their first novel, *The Darkest Lies*. Jan is a member of the Dramatists Guild.

Shannon Michal Dow is a national award-winning playwright whose works have been produced and received readings around the country. She has been literary manager of The Playwrights Collective of the Country Players of Brookfield, Connecticut, as well as a play analyst and acquisitions editor for a play publishing company. She gives playwriting workshops for adults and teenagers. Her full-length plays have been published by Samuel French and Popular Play Service.

She has been a feature writer and editor and a film and theatre reviewer for various Connecticut newspapers and has served as a judge for several playwriting competitions. Her articles have appeared in *Connecticut* magazine and other periodicals. She also has worked professionally as a theatre director as well as a graphic and scenic artist and designer for the theatre. She is a member of the Dramatist Guild (The School House Theatre Playwrights Workshop, Croton Falls, New York).

Phosphene Publishing Company publishes books and DVDs relating to literature, history, the paranormal, film, spirituality, and the martial arts.

For other great titles, visit
phosphenepublishing.com

www.ingramcontent.com/pod-product-compliance
Lightning Source LLC
Chambersburg PA
CBHW061445040426
42450CB00007B/1215